e-Learning

ε-Learning

Concepts and Practice

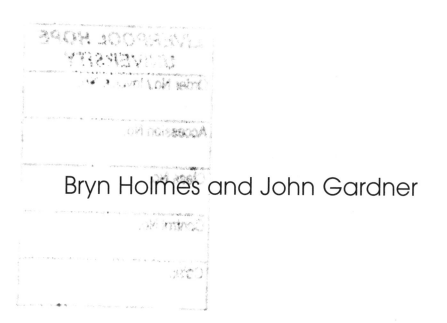

Bryn Holmes and John Gardner

SAGE Publications
Los Angeles • London • New Delhi • Singapore

First published 2006

Reprinted 2007

 SAGE Publications Ltd
1 Oliver's Yard
55 City Road
London EC1Y 1SP

SAGE Publications Inc.
2455 Teller Road
Thousand Oaks, California 91320

SAGE Publications India Pvt Ltd
B 1/I 1 Mohan Cooperative Industrial Area
Mathura Road, New Delhi 110 044
India

SAGE Publications Asia-Pacific Pte Ltd
33 Pekin Street #02-01
Far East Square
Singapore 048763

British Library Cataloguing in Publication data

A catalogue record for this book is available
from the British Library

ISBN 978-1-4129-1110-8
✓ ISBN 978-1-4129-1111-5 (pbk)

Library of Congress Control Number: 2005938636

Typeset by C&M Digitals (P) Ltd, Chennai, India
Printed and bound in Great Britain by TJ International, Padstow
Printed on paper from sustainable resources

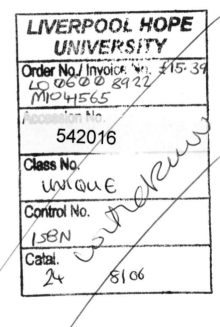

Contents

About the Authors

Bryn Holmes

Dr Bryn Holmes is an assistant professor in Educational Technology at Concordia University, Montreal. Her teaching and research interests encompass global perspectives of e-Learning, computer assisted language learning and e-Learning for special needs. She has taught on aspects of learning with technology in Japan, the UK, Ireland and Canada. Bryn has been extensively involved in EU projects with international partners. These have attracted funding in excess of 750,000 euro in the last five years and have explored the impact of technology on education across Europe as an underpinning theme. Bryn is also is the managing director of an Irish e-Learning company, Inishnet, that develops e-Learning environments for learners with visual impairments. Her project (as lead researcher), Accessible Communities for E-business funded by the European Union's Regional Innovative Actions programme, was selected as the most innovative in Ireland in 2004, by the South Eastern Regional Assembly (Ireland).

John Gardner

John is a professor in Education in the School of Education at Queen's University, Belfast. His main research areas include policy and practice in information technology and assessment in education. Since 1990, he has been principal investigator in over 20 large and small-scale projects involving over £1.6 million including research on student workstation usage in a university setting, using portable computers in school classrooms, virtual learning environments for schools and teachers' use of computers. His most recent project examined the feasibility of an electronic repository for education-related research reports and policy documents in Northern Ireland.

Preface

e-Learning Concepts and Practice is a book for anyone wishing to find out about e-Learning, or indeed find out where e-Learning is headed! We offer tutors and students alike the opportunity to develop their knowledge and understanding of e-Learning through a variety of Internet sources and related practical activities. Whether you are a tutor or student in a college, university or training organization, the structure of the book will take you through key aspects of e-Learning; from definition and design, to its applications and its future. Blogs, wikis and MOOs are explained and illustrated and we introduce and explain the new concepts of 'communal constructivism' and the 'Communal Yottaspace'.

We have carefully checked all the URLs and the websites we mention in the book, just before going to press, but the Internet as you may know is in a state of constant growth and change. If you cannot find a particular site then think about the key concepts that we are using to illustrate it and search for similar examples. In the same way, if you come across a word, phrase or concept that you do not understand, we encourage you to practise the skills we highlight in the text. We want you to e-Learn!

There are substantial dictionary and encyclopedia resources on the Web – some with free access, some with subscription access – and they are all easily accessed through any browser such as Internet Explorer or Firefox, or through any search engine such as Google or Yahoo! Search. One excellent source is Wikipedia – a free, communally constructed encyclopedia where anyone can create or contribute to a definition. On the basis that large numbers of people monitor and contribute to these definitions, the likelihood is that any errors will be ironed out. So if you have a query, we hope you will turn to the Web to answer it – but be careful, of course, some sources are much more reliable than others!

This book promotes communal constructivism, a concept of learning that has emerged as a strength of e-Learning. In communally constructed learning environments, each member of the community learns with and from others, and contributes learning resources for others. As a final word, therefore, we would be very remiss if we did not record our appreciation of the various colleagues and students in Inishnet, in Trinity College (Dublin), in Queen's (Belfast) and in Concordia (Montreal) with whom we have worked as part of our own community of learners in e-Learning.

Bryn Holmes and John Gardner
May 2006

List of Abbreviations

3D	three-dimensional
ABA	applied behaviour analysis
ACE	Accessible Communities for E-Business
ADA	Americans with Disabilities Act
ARPANET	Advanced Research Projects Agency Network
ASR	automatic speech recognition
BECTa	British Educational Communications and Technology Agency
BeST	electronic Basic Surgical Training
BETT	British Education Training and Technology
blog	weblog
CEN	European Standardization Committee
CENELEC	European Electrotechnical Standardization Committee
CERN	European Laboratory for Particle Physics
COL	Commonwealth of Learning
CoSE	Creation of Study Environments
CSS	cascading style sheet
D&P	drill and practice
EC	European Commission
ECDL	European Computer Driving Licence
ECDLPD	European Computer Driving Licence for People with Disabilities
EOE	Education Object Economy

ERIC	Education Resources Information Centre
ESO	European Standardization Organization
ETSI	European Telecommunications Standards Institute
EU	European Union
GIS	geographic information system
HCI	human–computer interface
HTML	HyperText Mark-up Language
HTTP	HyperText Transfer Protocol
H-NET	Humanities and Social Sciences Online
ICT	information and communication technology
IDeA	Improvement and Development Agency
IEEE	Institute of Electrical and Electronic Engineers
IEP	Individualized Education Program
IM	instant messaging
ITS	intelligent tutoring system
IVR	interactive voice response
LAN	local area network
LCSI	Logo Computer Systens Inc.
LIP	Learner Information Profile
LMS	learning management system
LSI	learning style inventory
MEP	Microelectronics Education Programme
MERLOT	Multimedia Educational Resource for Learning and Online Teaching
MLE	managed learning environment
MOO	multi-user dungeon object-oriented
MUD	multi-user dungeon
MuGame	multi-user variants of games
MuSim	multi-user variants of simulations
NASA	National Aeronautics and Space Administration
NCBI	National Council for the Blind in Ireland
NCET	National Council for Educational Technology
NDPCAL	National Development Programme for Computer Based Learning
N-I Tut	non-interactive tutorial
OU	Open University

PARC	Palo Alto Research Center
PBL	problem-based learning
PDA	personal digital assistant
PRISM	Publishing Requirements for Industry Standard Metadata
SAVI	Social Assistance for/with the Visually Impaired
SCORM	Sharable Content Object Reference Model
SCRAN	Scottish Cultural Resources across the Network
SI	System Internationale
TILE	The Inclusive Learning Exchange
TTS	text-to-speech synthesis
ULLeap	UL Lifelong Learner Information Profile
URL	universal resource locator
VICS	Visually-Impaired Computer Society of Ireland
VISUAL	Voice for Information Society Universal Access and Learning
VLE	virtual learning environment
VOIP	voice over Internet protocol
VXML	Voice eXtensible Mark-up Language
WAI	Web Accessibility Initiative
Web	World Wide Web
WIFI	Wireless Fidelity
WITSA	World Information Technology and Services Alliance
WYSIWYG	what you see is what you get
ZPD	zone of proximal development

1 Introduction

MISSION CRITICAL

e-Learning is unquestionably the major 'mission critical' in education systems the world over, and is likely to remain so for the foreseeable future. There are many reasons for it being so much in vogue, not least the globalization of commerce and citizenship, and the burgeoning of information and knowledge available on the Internet. The recognition that today's economies need to be knowledge based, which in turn require a workforce and consumer body that are characterized by flexibility, independence in learning and information and communications technologies competence, may be an even more compelling reason for governments to be as proactive as they are. As a means to increase access to learning – anytime and anywhere – the ensuing interest in e-Learning is nothing short of phenomenal, with the result that authoritative texts are in growing demand. No one could claim to offer a text that would be definitive in such a fast-moving environment but we offer *e-Learning: Concepts and Practice* as an all-round but sophisticated entrée to the power and potential of e-Learning, and the main approaches to delivering it. We draw on a wide variety of globally dispersed examples and, in order to help understand why it is in the form we currently know it, we also provide a potted history to chart e-Learning's evolution from its antecedents in programmed learning. The text should therefore prove of interest to the general reader and to students, academics and professionals working in the field of educational computing.

The twin goals of the book are to provide an overview of existing e-Learning approaches and a vision of the future. We specifically look at ways that e-Learning will optimize teaching and learning for academic researchers, trainers and educators, World Wide Web (Web) developers, resource content managers and those who have a general interest in e-Learning. The intention is to enhance understanding of the potential of e-Learning by covering all its important aspects in ways that explore, through practical examples, the implications of its use. The insights gained will act as a foundation for further exploration.

Each of the nine chapters explores a different feature associated with e-Learning, from learning enrichment to lifelong learning. The sequence of chapters is laid out in a manner that takes the reader from the more simple concepts of how to provide enrichment in the learning process to the more complex issues involved in building a community of learners. Promoting the knowledge these learners develop in turn creates a self-sustaining learning community.

A FRAMEWORK OF PRACTICE

Traditional books are arguably not an adequate vehicle for dealing with e-Learning in that the printed page has considerable limitations when it comes to illustrating its interactional features and power. The design of *e-Learning: Concepts and Practice* therefore allows for the main text of each chapter to address the concepts involved, while a variety of 'break-out boxes' provides readers with opportunities to look more practically at aspects of e-Learning through carefully chosen websites and online activities.

e-Learning requires different types of engagement, categorized in the framework of key practices or skills illustrated in the petals of the e-learning 'flower' in Figure 1.1. Note that the radial nature of the flower petals imply that there is no hierarchy in this framework. In any one instance, the practical activity undertaken by the learner may involve only one or perhaps several of the actions or skills denoted in the figure. While it might be possible to suggest levels of complexity to associate with the elements of this framework, it is likely that such a consideration will be irrelevant. It will be the actual context and the learner's needs and aspirations that will determine which practice or skill is appropriate.

A brief outline of these key practices is provided below.

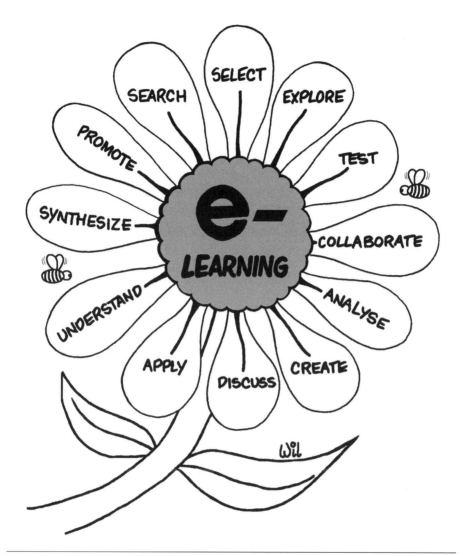

Figure I.I   A flower petal framework (non-hierachical) for e-Learning practices and skills

Searching and selecting

Usually in some combination, search and select activities are the 'bread and butter' of learners' collation of information; the one identifying where the sources of information might be (searching), the other choosing the most relevant sources according to the criteria established by their learning needs (selection). For example, the reader in Box 1.1 is asked to go the Massachusetts Institute of Technology's OpenCourseware site to search out and select specific academic materials from a wide range of resources for different subject areas. The final selection is made on the basis of the value of the courseware for their own purposes.

🖰 Box 1.1

Visit the Massachusetts Institute of Technology's OpenCourseware site at http://ocw.mit.edu/index.html and search for information on the poet John Donne. Select anything that would help you to develop your knowledge of the nature of English poetry in the sixteenth and seventeenth centuries. Do not worry if you have no interest in poetry – just try the exercise for fun.

Saving and keeping track of the information, and any new knowledge, are skills that will be challenged persistently by the sheer volume of material available. Bookmarking or saving favourite websites will make it easier to conduct subsequent searches, but personal annotated databases will be increasingly needed to hold all relevant electronic sources. There was a time when each family was lucky to have a few texts or perhaps only a Bible; today in the developed world we are literally drowning in information! The skills of criterion-searching and selecting by relevance are staples in the set of basic Internet literacy tools.

Exploring

Similar to searching, exploring implies a more relaxed browsing, looking for information that might match our interests or meet our needs. It is an almost everyday activity, as we scan a magazine or newspaper, for example, for items that interest us. As with searching, it is based on a set of criteria but more loosely than the specific search criterion ('information on John Donne') illustrated in Box 1.1.

Testing

Related to exploring is the discovery mode of e-Learning, in which learners try out ideas, test hypotheses, and so on. Web-based information comes in many forms and simulations, and games are examples in which the full potential of interactive engagement is used. Rather than simply reading new information, such activities enable the learner to avail him or herself of a type of information-cum-knowledge creation that requires them to explore and manipulate virtual circumstances and conditions relevant to the focus of their studies. For example, students of chemistry may test models of complex molecules or they may conduct virtual experiments. Social science students may model voting patterns or the factors affecting levels of poverty in specific regions. All such work proceeds in an e-Learning context without the burdens of expensive resources, real-time practicalities and, even, dangers that the real conditions might impose. The very act of 'doing' the work allows the learner to create and assimilate new knowledge. Have a go at Box 1.2!

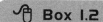 **Box 1.2**

Visit http://www.colorado.edu/physics/phet/simulations-base.html, which is a physics education site hosted by the University of Colorado. Use the Sound simulation to explore and test how sound is heard by a listener when the source experiences air pressure changes.

Analyse and synthesize

These activities often go together as learners deconstruct the complexity of a set of information (analyse) and rebuild it as their own knowledge (synthesize). When we analyse a set of information, be it train timetables or quotations for holiday insurance for example, we attempt to reduce it to different categories, distinguished by the importance we attach to each of them. Once we have looked at several versions of the information, the risks covered by each of several insurance policy proposals for example, we begin to synthesize it to make sure that what we eventually choose fits our needs and at a competitive cost within the options we have. Learning is no different. Whatever the context, the analysis of relevant information from different case studies, examples of scientific phenomena, periods of architecture or whatever, and the synthesis or pulling together of this information to suit our specific learning needs, are key learning skills necessary not only for constructing the new knowledge for ourselves, but for beginning to contribute new understandings for others. Have a look at the exercise in Box 1.3 – but do not worry, it is only an example and we do not expect you to complete the exercise!

🖰 Box 1.3

Check out the website of the Early Childhood Research and Practice online journal at http://ecrp.uiuc.edu/, and search through to find the following papers:

- The Llama Project (Ganzel and Stuglik, vol. 5, no. 2);
- The Lunch Project (Floerchinger, vol. 7, no. 1);
- The Construction Project (Berry and Allen, vol. 4, no. 1).

What are the common features of these project reports (Analyse) and what implications do they have for developing good practice in early years education (Synthesize)?

While the first six learning practices above assist learners to assimilate 'new knowledge and understanding', the next six exhort them to follow through, consolidate, share and use their knowledge gains.

Collaborate and discuss

The cycle might begin with the learners seeking to share the information and new knowledge with others (collaboration and discussion); a process that is well known to consolidate and improve understanding through the action of being obliged to explain (externalize) what has begun to be internalized. Very often we tell others about something we have read and a discussion ensues. One of the most powerful factors in promoting learning is this contribution to discussion and collaboration with others who are working towards the same goal. By articulating the ideas to others and hearing their inputs, by repeating them and teasing out the implications of theories or sets of conditions, such discussion will assist in formulating and consolidating new knowledge. In this way, connected learners can move each other beyond the level of superficial understandings.

Understand and apply

During this consolidation and sharing phase, it is likely that the learners will be faced with the challenges (or opportunities) to demonstrate their grasp of the new knowledge (understanding) by using it in context (applying it). This demonstration of understanding might be for the benefit of others but the major benefit accrues to the learners themselves. It is possible to apply knowledge blindly of course, with little understanding of the concepts and reasons for actions and outcomes. For example, the 'natural' snooker player may never reflect upon and understand the mathematical niceties of spin or cue-to-ball contact that make them champions. However, most people will benefit from training that explains and then practises the skills necessary to optimize these features of play. In many areas of life and work, action informed by understanding is generally more focused, efficient and, hopefully, successful. Taking basic information such as lecture notes or a literature review, and developing understanding through discussion, analysis and synthesis, will generally enable better and more purposeful application of the newly gained knowledge in solving problems or making decisions.

Create and promote

Once they are comfortable with their grasp of a learning context, learners may fashion their new knowledge in transferable forms (creating 'learning objects') to make it available to other learners in a communal learning resource space (promoting the learning objects they have created).

e-Learning offers unique opportunities to create new knowledge and to promote its use by others through the ease of communication and dissemination of the new knowledge, within a community of learners context. Indeed, this process is an explicit difference between the learning made possible with new technologies and the older, traditional models of learning, whether these might be the restrictive didacticism of teacher-led learning or the greater freedom of teacher-facilitated learning.

By knowledge, it must be emphasized, we do not mean merely facts or conceptual understanding. We also mean new ways of looking at existing knowledge, new insights to complex processes and access to the experience and expertise of others in relation to the context of the learning. With the vast amount of knowledge now available on the World Wide Web, it is reasonable to accept that methods of accessing, storing and retrieving information are now much more important aspects of the learning process than perhaps they have been in the past.

As knowledge is more and more easily constructed and disseminated, the learner nowadays is also called upon more often to judge its usefulness and, indeed, whether or not it is trustworthy and factual. Technical advances are making authoring and publishing tools easy to use, enabling learners to engage in sophisticated communication and interaction, between themselves and their various audiences (for example, their assessors or professional, academic and community groupings with an interest in their work). As new ways of looking at knowledge emerge, the ease and freedom of publishing on the Internet has resulted in an excellent environment for teachers to guide students in creating their own online classes for other learners – a true community of learners in which the learners provide resources and learning opportunities for their peer learners.

BLOOM'S TAXONOMY

Readers versed in education theory will no doubt recognize a resonance between the framework of e-Learning practices above (Analyse, Synthesize, and so on) and Bloom's Taxonomy (Bloom et al., 1956) of increasingly sophisticated intellectual skills, namely: Knowledge, Comprehension, Application, Analysis, Synthesis and Evaluation. The taxonomy retains considerable relevance today and, although it is often referred to as a hierarchy of skills, it was never meant to be seen as some form of sequence in which some skills are achieved before others, implying for example that 'apply' cannot come before 'comprehend'. Any notion that such a linear hierarchy could apply to learning situations in the twenty-first century is definitely a non-runner. Since Bloom's committee proposed the taxonomy in the 1950s there have been revolutionary changes in education brought about by a variety of developments. These include the rise of learner-centred educa-tion, the onset of mass education and, most importantly in more recent times, the phenomenal emergence of information and communications technologies in education.

In the 1950s only the most far-sighted of futurologists could have con-jured up the possibility of a learning resource as immense as the Internet, or the power of some of its search engines. Learners today, for example, have almost instant access to a search of over 8,000,000,000 (that is, 8 billion) Web pages courtesy of systems such as Google, with some 11.5 billion pages overall. On first encounter, most learners might see this solely as what we would call 'information noise'. In relation to this vast amount of available Knowledge, a *linear* trek through any hierarchy of skills, such as Bloom's taxonomy might suggest, will likely be disrupted by the need for Analysis before Application, for example, or the need for judgement (Evaluation – the highest skill in Bloom's taxonomy) from the initial search. Only through a *combination* of Knowledge, Analysis, Synthesis, Application, Evaluation and Comprehension, therefore, is it likely that learners will truly assimilate what they need as new knowledge. By the same token, only by an appro-priate combination of any two or more of the practices in Figure 1.1, will learning progress today.

It is not surprising that in the context of the very formal and didactic approaches to education in the 1950s, Bloom's committee did not explic-itly identify collaboration as another powerful facilitator of individual learn-ing. No criticism of them is intended, of course; their contribution to educational theory is immense. The connectivity of information and com-munication technologies today, however, is such that collaboration is not simply a casual social activity on the margins of learning; it is becoming more important in supporting thinking and assimilating new knowledge and understandings.

ε-LEARNING

If learning and learners have experienced major changes since Bloom's day, it is inevitable that schoolteachers, university lecturers and private sector trainers have been facing equally major changes in the way they approach their work. Tutors today are required to go beyond selecting a textbook for their students. Now they must regularly evaluate new resources; searching, selecting, evaluating, planning for, implementing and managing them in order to promote best practice in learning. e-Learning for many is the 'mission critical' and must be explored, first and foremost, from a learning perspective. An exploration of the state of the art of e-Learning is essentially, therefore, an examination of the most advanced features of information and communications technology that can support, create and deliver an educational experience. At its best, e-Learning offers new opportunities for both the educator and the learner to enrich their teaching and learning experiences through virtual environments that support not just the delivery, but also the exploration and application of information. Debate about the pros and cons of e-Learning is typically focused on a perceived lack of face-to-face contact. This has resulted in a mix of e-Learning and more conventional learning – a process entitled blended learning. Rather than having one type of learning experience mandated for them, learners should be able to have as much choice and selection as possible. There is a real need for a text on e-Learning that provides a solid foundation to the field but which also models some of the processes involved in the multi-faceted and multi-focus knowledge-building that is at the heart of the successful e-Learning experience. This book therefore seeks to present an overview of what e-Learning currently is and a vision of how it will develop in the future.

THE CHAPTERS

In designing this book's structure, therefore, we felt that readers would want to get straight into finding out what e-Learning is. The next chapter, 'Enter e-Learning', addresses this need by describing what e-Learning currently is, illustrated by a range of examples. Chapter 3, 'A potted history of e-Learning' charts the history of e-Learning for those who wish to know how it all came about while Chapter 4, 'e-Learning – an educational revolution' is on how e-Learning is set to revolutionize still further our approaches to learning. Who is e-Learning? What are they e-Learning? When and where are they e-Learning? These are questions that this chapter addresses.

Chapter 5, 'e-Learning theory – communal constructivism' then looks at how learning theory is coping with the new modes of learning and the wider concept of the learner that has evolved in recent times. At the heart of this chapter, 'communal constructivism' is presented as the key extension to socio-constructivist theory to underline e-Learning. Communal constructivism is an extension of modern learning theory's most central idea, in which learners construct and assimilate their own knowledge from their own learning opportunities. Within the networked communication world that e-Learning provides, it is a natural step to the formation of communities of individual learners pursuing the same goals. From there the next step is to learn as a community; constructing and sharing knowledge at a community level in a form of social constructivism. Communal constructivism takes this yet another step further by identifying a process in which the learners involved deliberately contribute their own learning to a community resource base for the benefit of their peers and future learners.

Chapter 6, 'e-Learning design – concepts and considerations', examines how e-Learning activities and resources can enrich the learning experience and how they can be used to scaffold students' thinking, to integrate critical thinking skills and to provide 'cognitive apprenticeships' which furnish the learner with opportunities to engage with experts in the subject of their learning. 'Empowered learners – powerful tools for learning' is the subject of Chapter 7 and focuses on how a variety of design features for e-Learning, for example in terms of layout and navigation, have been used to maximize learners' opportunities to manage the growing communal knowledge space. There are problems of course, such as copyright in relation to learning objects created by others, and these too are aired. A number of examples, which will include students' use of wireless networks in lectures to surf for more detailed notes, are used to highlight the potential and the issues involved.

The key themes of Chapter 8, 'e-Learning – learner emancipation', are the accessibility and impact of e-Learning on communities of learners who experience special access difficulties. e-Learning is, of course, a highly visual learning environment and to make it amenable to those without sight or with partial sight is one the greatest challenges there is. Chapter 8 addresses this challenge with examples that can be extended to other groups with special needs.

The final chapter, 'e-Learning – endless development?', concludes the tour of the concepts and practice in e-Learning by looking to the future to try to establish where the new developments in e-Learning might be. Indeed, the question is posed: is there an end in sight to e-Learning developments? The creation of self-generating and self-sustaining e-communities can only extend opportunities for their members and, ultimately, global society as a whole to continue learning and to build the knowledge base for new learners as they continuously come on-stream. The technological and infrastructural developments of today, such as nano-technologies, the Semantic Grid and emerging communal learning tools such as wikis and blogs, underpin the argument that we are looking at a future that will provide anywhere (mobile and ubiquitous) and anytime online access for every citizen to an almost inconceivably huge knowledge and learning space. In Chapter 9 we give this phenomenon a name: the 'Communal Yottaspace' of knowledge (where 'yotta' is the largest defined number in the Systeme Internationale of measurement, 10^{24}).

So where to first? We have named Chapter 2. 'Enter e-Learning' as a means of establishing the backdrop for the rest of the text. The initial focus is the perhaps obvious question: why do we have e-Learning? A definition is offered and developed on the basis of an exploration of the key aspects of learning and e-Learning, and how the convergence between them is progressing. The benefits of e-Learning are argued and the challenges and opportunities surrounding its use are explored.

Enter e-Learning

WHY DO WE HAVE e-LEARNING?

Arguably this is a question that does not need to be asked! So many of our day-to-day activities are now routinely technology-based, for example electronic access to cash or shopping, that for a large majority if not all of us techno-familiarity is a necessity. Many people, however, remain on the other side of the 'digital divide', isolated by such factors as socio-economic circumstances, disability or simply a lack of interest, perhaps through personal choice or other cultural influence. Electronic purchasing and information searching is all around us, and becoming more and more pervasive. For example, the word 'google' has become an everyday verb used to describe electronic searching, regardless of whether Google itself is the search engine being used (see *Webster's New Millennium Dictionary*, 2005). Such is the pervasiveness of technology-based activities across society that there are few governments that do not have information technology-related learning programmes as part of their national educational policies. For the most part, these promote learning *about* the technology, how to use it and how to benefit from it. For some 40 years now, however, since the first major developments in using computers to deliver drill and practice in the 1960 and 1970s, one of the most widely acknowledged benefits has been the many uses for computers in delivering education and facilitating learning. Whether it is learning in schools, universities or the workplace, appropriately designed e-Learning approaches to any aspect of a target curriculum can provide significant opportunities for learners to create and acquire knowledge for themselves.

e-LEARNING DEFINED

There may be as many definitions of e-Learning as there are academic papers on the subject, but broadly speaking they focus on the same set of features. Take the European e-Learning Action Plan definition as an example: 'the use of new multimedia technologies and the Internet to improve the quality of learning by facilitating access to resources and services as well as remote exchanges and collaboration' (COM, 2001: 2). Here we have mention of electronic technologies, as vehicles for education services and resources, and as the conduits for collaboration and communication. If we may be so bold as to focus on the essentials, however, our preferred definition would view e-Learning simply as:

> *online access to learning resources, anywhere and anytime.*

New opportunities, new learning environments

e-Learning offers new opportunities for both educators and learners to enrich their teaching and learning experiences, through virtual environments that support not just the delivery but also the exploration and application of information and the promotion of new knowledge. The focus for any exploration of the state-of-the art of e-Learning is therefore no more and no less than the combination and convergence of the most advanced features of digital information and communication technologies, for example, live broadcasts, mobile video and audio telecommunications, three-dimensional (3D) graphics, email, the Web and object-oriented interfaces, all of which can be designed to support, create and deliver significant educational experiences and environments. Concerns about a lack of face-to-face contact have given rise in some contexts to a mix of e-Learning, which may be 'at a distance', and more conventional face-to-face learning in the classroom; a process entitled 'blended learning'. e-Learning enables learners to have as much choice as is practically and economically possible.

e-Learning takes place in online environments that range from providing information to engaging the learner in complex interactive simulations. Managed learning environments have been developed to provide an electronic solution to managing the complexity not just of the learning environment (resources, online tutorials, discussion groups, assignment submissions, and so on) but also of the records of the learners' biographical details, examinations and assessment profiles, and the courses they have taken. Very often the students will have access to all this information through unique personal identifiers, while those who facilitate their learning (teachers, lecturers and so on), and those who administer it, will also have appropriate access privileges. Within the learning environment, the students can learn together in e-communities, for example in virtual learning environments (VLEs) or multi-use object-oriented environments (MOOs – more about these later). Interaction is supported by 'asynchronous' communication tools such as email and discussion boards – where 'asynchronous' simply means that they are not happening in the same time frame. An email, for example, is a one-way communication that can be answered immediately or later in a one-way response when the receiver reads it. 'Synchronous' tools, such as chat rooms and shared whiteboards, offer the immediacy of two-way communication and are also powerful vehicles for the interaction that the learning environment supports. The learning experience itself can be very varied, perhaps involving the student in lectures provided by video, in manipulating simulations or in interrogating an expert system. By virtue of the medium, the learning activities can be tracked and assessed using online tools which are also embedded in the environment.

Information is everywhere, sometimes more accessible than at other times. For example, compare the information disseminated freely by organizations through their websites with the information stored by organizations which have to be forced to make it available to the citizens who 'own' it. Access is often through legal devices such as the Freedom of Information Acts in the UK and the USA, the Data Protection Act in the UK and the Privacy Act in the USA. Technology has allowed the creation and dissemination of information on an unprecedented scale and with unprecedented ease. Government has expanded to e-government, commerce has expanded to e-commerce – and learning has in turn expanded to e-Learning. Technological advances have extended the dimensions of the information used and provided by social institutions (government, commerce, leisure, education and so on) and have revolutionized the processes that make the information meaningful or amenable for professionals and ordinary consumers alike. The synergy between the technology and the information owners and providers has released the potential for an information-rich personalized resource for every person; a resource that is actually a huge globally connected learning environment.

Personalized access to community knowledge

Not everyone appreciates the potential for such a personalized resource, indeed arguably very few do. A major challenge we face today, therefore, is to create a desire in people to learn; and to foster and facilitate this desire throughout their lives. More and more often our individual desires for learning are being addressed in a learning community that becomes apparent as soon as we begin to search the Internet for resources. Think of the person who wishes to learn the best methods of growing strawberries or how to landscape their garden. Typing the questions 'What is the best way to grow strawberries?' and 'How do I design a garden?' into Yahoo Search or Ask Jeeves will each produce hundreds of thousands of potentially helpful links. Some will be courses of study, some will be advice published by gardening organizations and some will be forums to which like-minded people have addressed similar questions. These forums very often allow the searcher to avail him or herself of a collective response from those who have the necessary experience and expertise. But remember, judgement is a key skill in the e-Learning framework of practices. There is always the possibility that the advice given may not be appropriate to the circumstances envisaged or, indeed, may simply be incorrect.

In time, membership of common interest, e-Learning communities will become more common for many people, with an ever-expanding reservoir of resources that will provide an alternative to classroom-based learning. Hands-on and face-to-face contact will remain key approaches to making learning a grounded experience but working with and learning from others in an e-Learning context will allow greater access and a greater choice of resources. Additionally, there will be the potential for making each person's newly created knowledge available to new and existing learners. The use of e-Learning will continue to evolve and there is a need to ensure that good learning practices are at its core.

LEARNING FOR ALL

This book is fundamentally about learning for all, and as the twenty-first century progresses the sense that everyone is a learner will become more embedded in social discourse without any stigma of somehow being inadequate, as is sometimes the lot of the 'learner driver' for example! But e-Learning means that learners now and in the future will have opportunities to be tutors also. Giving people the opportunity to reinvest in learning environments is a form of communal constructivism (Holmes et al., 2001), a process in which learners put their learning back into the community to benefit others, which will promote an evolution of learning and teaching. Enriching and expanding the available learning opportunities will be important as everyone is constantly called upon to learn and create new knowledge, learn new ways of doing things and, at a deeper level, new ways of learning itself. Traditionally children of farmers learned agricultural skills, tradespeople passed on skills in weaving or woodwork and so on. As far back as 1976, the then UK Prime Minister, James Callaghan, famously argued in his Ruskin Speech that schools should meet the needs of their students in preparing them for the workplace as well as meeting their needs in personal development: 'There is no virtue in producing socially well-adjusted members of society who are unemployed because they do not have the skills … Nor at the other extreme must they be technically efficient robots' (Callaghan, 1976).

Today it is very unlikely that the first job young people might be trained to do, when they join the workforce for the first time, will be the one they have for the rest of their working lives. Society has experienced such rapid changes in social and economic circumstances that the education system has been left behind, despite Callaghan's and subsequent governments' interventions. Specifically, students and teachers find themselves with new things to learn and do but with a dearth of new ways of learning and doing them. As the US government-backed Partnership for 21st Century Skills put it: 'There remains, however, a profound gap between the knowledge and skills most students learn in school and the knowledge and skills they need in typical 21st century communities and workplaces. … Today's education system faces irrelevance unless we bridge the gap between how students live and how they learn' (2003: 3). The push is on to make learning environments more relevant to today's students and e-Learning offers one of the most important ways forward.

The wide array of jobs now open to people means that schools and universities have to provide curricula that specifically arm them with generic skills such as numeracy, literacy, communication, working with others and technological literacy. The limited, subject-based curricula of yesteryear cannot deliver these to the necessary level, with the consequence that the call for lifelong learning supported by new information and communication technologies has become widespread. Increasingly, learning is about preparing students to think, both quickly and well: 'The knowledge society will need graduates who want to learn throughout their lives and can be flexible and creative as well as problem solve. Technical skills and "information finding" skills are also key' (Scardamalia and Bereiter, 1996).

When memorization was a dominant educational technique, assessment was relatively easy. With a new focus on encouraging learners to develop skills better suited to the information age, judging what those skills are, delivering them and then testing them – all in an online environment – presents huge challenges.

Cross-cultural contexts

Computer-based approaches to learning do not come cheap. In both the UK and the USA, huge sums of money have been invested in all aspects of the technology and its integration in education. In the European Union as a whole, massive funds and resources have been dedicated to researching the present role and future potential for e-Learning and digital content delivery. Understandably, supporting cross-cultural initiatives and promoting collaborative e-Learning environments, in the context of a wide variety of cultures, languages, educational systems and training needs, is of particular interest to the expanding European community and will prove to be an important testing ground. The priority is therefore reflected in the budget: 16 billion euros (approximately £11 billion or US$20 billion) allocated for a new generation of European programmes in education and culture from 2007–2013:

> Europe's future economy and society are being formed in the classrooms of today. Students need to be both well educated in their chosen field and digitally literate if they are to take part effectively in tomorrow's knowledge society. e-Learning – the integration of advanced information and communication technologies (ICT) into the education system – achieves both aims. (eEuropa, 2005)

> ### 🖱 Box 2.1
>
> Check out Journey North (http://www.learner.org/jnorth), which is a cross-cultural and cross-national project that aims to break down barriers through connecting students across cultures, a continent and three countries: Mexico, the USA and Canada. Students in all three countries collect data relating to different insect and animal migrations and signs of spring. The system seeks to promote understanding by enabling the students to share and discuss their field observations. A variety of species are followed in their annual migrations, including monarch butterflies, bald eagles, robins, hummingbirds and whooping cranes, and there is a study of the emergence in spring of various plants such as tulips. The site has well-developed supporting resources and training for teachers.

ε-LEARNING RESOURCES

Economies of scale in the late 1980s dictated that increasingly the IBM MS-DOS based business machines dominated the market while computers designed for playing video games, such as the Atari, have given way to today's Sony Playstations and Microsoft Xboxes. e-Learning, as a result, now takes place in the surviving office-oriented personal computers that have dominated the computer market. The 'teaching machine' came to be, by default, the personal computer and educational software compatible with the Microsoft Windows or Mac Os operating systems that began to proliferate. There is such an overwhelming number of titles at present that it is often difficult for educators at secondary and primary levels of education to choose appropriate packages. The annual British Education and Training Technology (BETT) exhibition, for example, which is billed as the leading UK educational technology trade event, provides a platform for over 550 educational computing software and related hardware suppliers.

In the UK the large amount of software specifically targeted at school subjects is partly due to the economy of scale created by the National Curriculum and partly due to government investment. There is, for example, a planned £500 million investment to deliver twenty-first century facilities in primary schools by 2009–10, and £50 million to support the provision of information and communications technologies for the most disadvantaged students over the period 2006–08 (HM Treasury, 2005: 133). To assist teachers in choosing appropriate learning packages for their classes, the British Educational Communications and Technology Agency (BECTa) has created an online Educational Software Database (http:// besd.becta.org.uk/) where software is described and reviewed by schoolteachers for schoolteachers, and where possible is linked to reviews on the software from another support site: Teachers Evaluating Educational Multimedia at http://www.teem.org.uk/. For universities the Higher Education Academy offers a resource area on e-learning and in 2005 launched a benchmarking exercise to provide a set of standards for e-Learning (http://www.heacademy.ac.uk/)

The *raison d'être* of the Internet is to link computers all over the world and to enable access to the digital information for which they act as servers. Hepp et al. (2004) argue that issues surrounding the use of digital content have moved from a generalist approach to an evermore detailed one: from an initial examination of online classrooms in the early 1990s to the potential of digital content to improve tutors' practice and the effectiveness of learning. There is at present a move towards developing, exchanging and using learning objects, specifically interoperable and modular digital resources, which we turn to again in Chapter 7.

The online lists of research resources of the early 1990s have also evolved into increasingly sophisticated information repositories. Take for example the Gutenberg collection of online books. Project Gutenberg is one of the oldest private initiatives to support education using networked computers. The initiative was started in 1971 by Michael Hart to make copyright-free books available electronically. He essentially invented the first e-book.

🖱 Box 2.2

Visit the Project Gutenberg site and consider whether you could volunteer to upload a book at http://www.gutenberg.org/ or try the Australian Project Gutenberg for a flavour of 'down-under' approaches to the concept (http://gutenberg.net.au/). If you have programming skills, consider helping to mark up documents in XHTML

(Continued)

or XML, making e-books easily read and printed out, as well as opening them up to searching and analysis. Visit the HTML Gutenberg Writers' Guild at http://gutenberg.hwg.org/.

Communication tools

A wide variety of communication tools can be used to support teaching and learning. For example, learning has been taking place via email, either formally or informally through newsgroups and online bulletin boards (BBS) for over 30 years. Such simple text-based information sharing is still a popular means of communication today, especially with those using older technologies or in areas served by low bandwidth communications technology. Over this time though, e-Learning environments have evolved to specialize in the provision of tools that enable users to express themselves in increasingly sophisticated ways. Systems that allow the screen to speak (screen readers for the visually impaired) or which symbolize non-verbal actions are becoming more common. Support tools such as virtual whiteboards, sharable text documents, Web page projection and transcript recorders are also adding to the communications repertoire.

Internet telephony is being hailed as the latest and possibly most aggressive 'disruptive' technology. According to the leader in *The Economist* of 17 September 2005, the voice over Internet protocol (VOIP) is set to 'cause revenue from voice calls to wither away' (*Economist*, 2005: 11). The article continues: 'It is now no longer a question of whether VOIP will wipe out traditional telephony, but a question of how quickly it will do so. People in the industry are already talking about the day, perhaps only five years away, when telephony will be a free service …'. The article quotes Niklas Zennstom, the co-founder of the main VOIP provider, Skype, as saying 'you should not have to pay for making phone calls in the future, just as you don't pay to send email' and makes the ominous observation that VOIP means the 'slow death of the trillion-dollar voice telephony market'. Much of our communications in the future are therefore likely to be VOIP based, with the protocol eventually extending to multi media. This in turn will greatly reduce the access costs to e-Learning as broadband systems provide interactive services at much reduced costs to the learner than exist today.

Box 2.3

Explore the facilities offered by the Internet telephony system, Skype at http://www.skype.com/helloagain.html. You can try free conferencing using the desktop software application which can be downloaded from the site. Skype's founders, Niklas Zennström and Janus Friis, were the original creators of Kazaa, the peer-to-peer music download site. To take full advantage of online telephone conferencing you will need a webcam(era), a microphone and headphones.

Email remains the most popular method of communicating online and is such an embedded feature of today's society that it is difficult to think how we would fare without it. Even in its earliest days, email was quickly exploited to support learning. For example, text-based email environments and discussion forums have supported language learning for many years. Increasingly, the supporting information is moving onto the Web where online centralized data capture makes it much easier to trace the history of any specific email or 'conversation' so as to review or reflect on the learning. Staying with the language learning context, the European Commission's e-Tandem initiative is an example of an e-Learning system that brings together language learners for collaborative learning. The Tandem Language Learning Partnerships for Schools (1998–2000) was a project which supported student exchanges of email between schools and teacher training institutions in France, Germany, Great Britain, Italy and Spain. It then evolved into the eTandem system of today, which enables learners to exchange emails half in their own language and half in the language they wish to learn.

Box 2.4

Interested in improving your language abilities? Why not explore the eTandem Europe site at http://www.slf.ruhr-uni-bochum.de/etandem/etproj-en.html. Choose a partner and test the possibilities of collaborative learning online!

Video communications

Video-conferencing is still emerging as a means of communication, incorporating broadcasts through microwave technology or Internet-based streamed video techniques using two-way compressed video and television. However, as potential learners' access to high bandwidth increases there will be more opportunities to deliver fully fledged courses and seminars, or to conduct meetings and brainstorming sessions. Even as it stands, there is considerable use of inexpensive low-end video-conferencing, using a webcam, microphone and speakers.

⌂ Box 2.5

Technology is continually evolving and e-Learning approaches are supporting increasingly rich means of facilitating learning on a wide geographic base. For an example, explore the video demos on Stanford University's Stanford Online site at http://scpd.stanford.edu/scpd/about/delivery/. Stanford uses this facility to transmit its classes, within two hours of them finishing, locally through television and worldwide through compressed video. Students can also interact asynchronously with the lecturer and other students through email and chat-room facilities.

Role-playing games

Role-playing games have also played a major part in the emergence of highly engaging and innovative e-Learning environments. In the earliest days, these games were played by email or through bulletin boards while nowadays they are often distributed as stand-alone CD-ROM packages or played by many users simultaneously over the Internet. 'Dungeons and Dragons' is the most well known of the games, which typically combine role play and problem-solving, and is reputed to have been a major influence in the development of what are now called multi-user dungeons or MUDs. The first online MUD is credited as having been developed by Roy

Trubshaw and Richard Bartle at the University of Essex in 1978. Online MUDs allow players from across the world to become dungeon masters and each player is represented by an avatar – a graphical representation of the character they play. The MUD's providers or publishers host the game's environment or 'persistent world' that the players inhabit.

The extension to the MUD concept, literally the multi-user dungeon object-oriented system, a MOO, has been used in a variety of ways to good effect, for example in language learning. In e-Learning the basis of the environment is the same as a MUD, that is, the learners take on roles and have 'avatars' act them out in the 'reality' of the virtual environment that the MOO allows to be created. The SchMOOze University, created by Julie Falsetti at the City University of New York is an example of a MOO that provides a virtual environment for non-native English speakers to practise interaction in English. The environment is modelled on a university campus and there is a variety of tasks to do, including a treasure hunt to complete, with all activities requiring engagement with the target language.

🖰 Box 2.6

Go to the schMOOze University site at http://schmooze.hunter. cuny.edu/ and explore the basic MOO commands. You should also have a look at the schMOOze newspaper. To get a flavour of a MOO world follow the link 'Interview with a Cat' to Michael Guest's experience with schMOOze.

Activeworlds Inc. is an example of a provider that has focused on creating and delivering 3D content on the Internet. The ActiveWorlds online environment offers users the chance to build their own 3D world and very often such environments are used for online chat. Careful vetting is always prudent, therefore, before any tutor, and especially a teacher of younger children, takes a class online. Activeworlds offer a separate 'Educational Universe' at http://www.activeworlds.com/edu/index.asp, which is dedicated to supporting the use of their technology in virtual learning environments.

Virtual learning environments

Although virtual learning environments (VLEs) can be considered to include MOOs and MUDs, they are often conceived as ends in themselves or additions to regular classroom activity, sometimes influenced by and in turn influencing the online gaming communities. An example of a VLE for schoolteachers is TappedIn at http://www.tappedin.com. TappedIn is a web-based multi-user virtual environment that is set up to have the look and feel of an actual college campus, with an integrated set of tools to support communication and collaboration. Members can create their own office spaces, including such features as virtual shared whiteboards. The environment is specifically designed for educators and allows teachers to create their own teaching spaces and offices with friendly features such as 'sticky notes' for posting welcome messages, agendas and so on. When people communicate in the TappedIn environment, transcripts are automatically emailed to them and messages can be saved for those not logged in. TappedIn staff also provide a newsletter and regular online 'training sessions' on how to use its features and so on. Another system, the Creation of Study Environments, based at the University of Staffordshire (CoSE at http://www.staffs.ac.uk/COSE/), sets out quite deliberately to be learner-centred with a design based on constructivist principles. Tutors initially create the study environments for their course groups. The students then access all available resources for selection to their own 'basket' and can create their own materials for addition to the resources. The link between assessment and learning activity is made clear and a management system enables monitoring of progress, activity logging, assignment submission and receipt issuing, tests and storage of results and so on (see more about such managed systems below).

Simulations

Simulations are also a major element in some e-Learning systems, with some links to gaming, though they are generally less likely to involve competition between learners. At university level, gaming may be used to increase motivation for simulations where participants impact on the outcome through informed decision-making. Consider SimCity (http://simcity.ea.com/) where students build a virtual city. Prudent municipal management demands that they attend to such matters as city finances, public services, land zoning for business and residential needs, and so on. The more exciting elements of the 'job' arise when natural disasters strike or there is civil unrest with citizens rioting and major disruption. In one UK example of its classroom use (BBC News, 2005), teachers and schoolchildren in Gillingham have teamed up with the software makers to create a special version complete with recognizable local landmarks. The students use the game to redesign their home town, and so learn about environmental and transport issues.

A simulation can assist in turning information into knowledge as learners are given the opportunity to apply what they know and see the results. The use of animations can help in understanding complex concepts in such subjects as physics and biology, and simulations take this a step further by allowing the interaction of the concepts and processes to be illustrated and controlled by the student. Simulations can also be used when it is very costly to make mistakes while learning, such as in training pilots and doctors. 'Virtual medical schools' have also become important and quite sophisticated, partly because the medical training sector is relatively well funded and partly because of the increasing use of technology in medical research and surgery itself. One such example is the 'electronic Basic Surgical Training system' (BeST) at http://www.rcsi.ie/best/, an initiative arising from a collaboration between the Royal College of Surgeons of Ireland and Harvard Medical School. It almost goes without saying that in fields where technology is causing rapid change in professional practice itself, e-Learning environments are likely to be both cutting edge and highly relevant. Instead of simulations of operations, for example, there are huge benefits to be had from doctors being able to operate on patients at a distance, using the latest in miniature camera technologies, while their students view the actual operation, and interact with them, from any corner of the globe.

Learning management systems

Online, Internet-based learning management systems (LMSs, sometimes called managed learning environments, MLEs or integrated learning systems,

ILSs) are specifically designed to deliver teaching programmes. They provide shells to populate with course content and offer a variety of course delivery methods. Students can access resource materials, interact with the lecturer and collaborate with peers. For many educationalists they represent the epitome of what an e-Learning environment is today. In terms of design they are more sophisticated and larger-scale variants of the personal computer or local area network (LAN)-based integrated learning systems, with online facilities for course enrolment, progress monitoring, tests and student record-keeping. Like their LAN-based cousins, many provide ways to measure and record student activity, the amount of time each student spends logged on, the receipt of assignments and the students' performances in assignments and tests. The main distinction between the online and non-online systems in most cases is that the online versions generally allow the tutors to 'author' the virtual learning environments in which the students work. The best known systems are those from Blackboard and WebCT (http://www.webct.com/).

🖱 Box 2.7

Explore the Blackboard (http://www.blackboard.com) and WebCT (http://www.webct.com/) sites and search for demos of the systems and their facilities. EduTools, http://www.edutools.info/about/index. jsp is an open resource for the worldwide higher education community and provides independently reviewed analyses of selected course management software tools.

Though expensive, these systems are the market leaders in university online course delivery and offer sophisticated authoring tools (with ready-made modules for student 'drop-boxes', discussion forums, record storage and so on), ease of navigation and robust operation. Aside from some proprietary systems (such as CoSE above), 'open source' initiatives in course management software, such as PostNuke (http://www.postnuke.com), are increasingly promoting low-cost or free alternatives where specific features can be fitted together (such as a calendar and a discussion board) into a custom-built environment. Others such as Moodle (http://moodle.org/) offer a full e-Learning environment for educational and training institutions, which can be easily downloaded and customized.

🖱 Box 2.8

Visit the Moodle site (http://moodle.org/) and compare it with the information you found out about Blackboard and WEbCT in Box 2.7. Consider the information from all three systems and take a view on which system might be best for your needs.

Open source systems, like Moodle, may be less tested and less robust than the large-scale commercial alternatives, but they often offer more opportunity for tailoring to specific needs and freedom for experimentation.

Learning management systems are often built to emulate the traditional learning and teaching structures and processes of schools and universities (the more familiar they are, the less intimidating a prospect for the staff to take on), and as such they have not sought to push out the boundaries of what online learning could be. Universities often see benefits in lecturers freeing up additional time for research by exploiting the reduction in administration of teaching that a learning management system can offer. Lecturers also appreciate the structure and ease of access to resources that the systems offer. Training organizations may also find that the traditional delivery structure and design of the learning management system assists them in making their programmes more efficient and accessible to all their clients, wherever they might be.

However much tutors may initially enjoy the benefits of having their lectures located in a highly structured and accessible online environment for their students, they may ultimately come to feel that such managed environments can prove restrictive to innovation and impulse in the course delivery. There are also some fundamental questions to be asked about the role of tutors. If all of their lecture content and support notes are available over the Internet, are they themselves actually needed? Simply reading lectures leads to empty lecture halls. Will the online availability of the full notes do the same? In institutions using lecture-driven models of delivery, there are signs that this is the case. For teachers in schools and tutors in training organizations this may be less of a problem if e-Learning is blended with other classroom activities. e-Learning can optimize the learning experience by providing a variety of different ways of embodying the concepts being studied and encompassing the culture of the discipline. This should therefore free tutors from repetitive and mundane information delivery-type teaching loads and, hopefully, allow them to focus on imparting higher-level skills through tutorial and other small-group interaction. These and other emerging issues, such as intellectual copyright on online course content, will be considered in later chapters.

As technology evolves and development in each type of e-Learning explored here continues to overlap, virtual learning environments and their overarching learning management systems will emerge as the core of a wider variety of customizable tools, especially those that suit flexible and mobile learning. Such environments, however, seem content to replicate 'real' campuses without really exploring what a virtual campus could be. This is a restriction that they must break out of if major advances are to be made. Emulating the traditional model of institutionalized teaching and learning as they do, they are somewhat like early television, which was essentially filmed radio; an example of a medium yet to develop its own discourse.

BENEFITS OF e-LEARNING

Computer-based educational approaches, and specifically e-Learning, have the potential to impact positively on the entire spectrum of education, and it is worth pausing to consider the nature of this impact through the following questions:

- Who is to be given the opportunity to be an e-Learner?
- What is to be e-Learned?
- How will learners engage with e-Learning?
- Where and when will learners engage with e-Learning?

Let us look briefly at these questions in turn.

Who is to be given the opportunity to learn through e-Learning?

At present there are examples of all categories of people – students, trainees, lifelong learners, and so on – using e-Learning. Advocates of e-Learning envisage the social penetration of e-Learning in the future to be wider and deeper, that is, with increasing numbers of people availing themselves of increasingly better quality learning opportunities. Learners who are disadvantaged as well as those with specific learning disabilities should not be left behind. e-Learning can ensure that no one is excluded from education by geographic, physical or social circumstance.

What is to be e-Learned?

This is a question for which it is easy to offer a general answer: for example, any learning needs can be accommodated through an e-Learning approach. However, it is very difficult to answer specifically as, clearly, the specifics will always depend on the individual learner's needs. Knowledge acquisition is undoubtedly essential for workforces to flourish and economies to expand, and good quality education provision is necessary to sustain a stable and fulfilling social structure. Defining what is to be learned by citizens or workers, however, is increasingly difficult. As the pace of change in society increases, it is flexible thinkers who can analyse and create new information that are needed, rather than experts in particular subjects and fields, whose expertise may well lose its currency as social and knowledge-related developments force changes. Clearly, however, all will not be lost for the 'experts' who can mediate developments for others less expert, in the particular field of their expertise. As different sectors of society and the economy will have different rates of developing and acquiring new and essential knowledge, there will be a continuing need for expert guidance in online knowledge mediation and its use.

How will learners engage with e-Learning?

Models of online learning that encourage learners to seek out information, evaluate it, share it collaboratively and, ultimately, transform it into their own knowledge will provide the best e-Learning spaces. The clear dilemma and major challenge here is to ensure that learners can access such flexible methods against a backdrop in which traditional models of learning have focused on teaching to a set of standards, rather than encouraging individually centred growth. Rapid change may be a constant feature of society but opportunities must be found to allow people to learn and exert influence on any new development. Appropriately designed, learner-centred and constructivist modes of e-Learning have the potential to assist learners to plan for and cope with significant changes in their lifestyle and workplaces.

Where and when will learners engage with e-Learning?

As physical limitations on access to information are removed, learning is increasingly taking place in locations selected by learners and at a time that suits their needs. The benefits of learning in the home will not only be obvious to today's learners but will likely have a positive impact on future generations. Flexibility in the location for learning also importantly means the inclusion of those who are least mobile, such as children in hospital, and those who are most mobile, such as aircraft pilots. The answer to the question, as in the definition we adopted, is that e-Learning allows people to learn anytime, anywhere!

e-Learning can greatly enhance the quality of the education through:

- contributing to an evolution in the way students learn;
- enriching and extending the learning experience of students;
- providing powerful tools for learners to exploit the World Wide Web;
- contributing to the evolution of theories of learning;
- opening up learning to students who might otherwise be restricted through disadvantage or impairment.

There are many considerations in assessing the extent to which e-Learning can achieve these lofty goals.

CHALLENGES AND OPPORTUNITIES

Many researchers suggest that the use of computers in schools has moved the classroom culture closer to that of an 'ideal classroom'. Such claims and their underpinning assumptions are rarely questioned but some writers such as Larry Cuban do not brook any rose-tinted perspectives. His two publications, 'Computers meet classroom: classroom wins' (1993) and *Oversold and Underused: Computers in the Classroom* (2001), very much challenge the status quo on educational computing. He underpins his scepticism with empirical data. For example, he reports that in a recent study of schools in the computer-rich 'Silicon Valley' in California: 'less than 5 percent of teachers integrated computer technology into their curriculum and instructional routines' (Cuban, 2001: 133). In fact 'the overwhelming majority of teachers employed the technology to sustain existing patterns of teaching rather than to innovate' (2001: 134). Such experience is not a one-off and educational computing certainly faces a number of struggles in schools. Necessity, however, is a well-known driver of innovation. In higher education, for example, the integration of information and communications technologies is seen as a significant, albeit partial solution for dealing with government policies that aim to have more than 50 per cent of all school leavers attending university. The opportunities and benefits perceived for e-Learning, such as increased efficiency of delivery and wider accessibility to learning, are ringing the changes in the academic sector, and also in the professional training sector.

In schools, however, the older 'tried and tested' models of teaching and learning continue to hold considerable sway, and the response to e-Learning initiatives remains comparatively muted. e-Learning environments demand that course management, design procedures and protocols need to be developed to shift the emphasis in teaching towards student engagement and peer support. There is therefore a clear need for leadership from school managers to espouse and promote the view that e-Learning can considerably enhance learning for their students. However, integrating e-Learning into normal practice is not a process that can be taken lightly. Its introduction can place significantly increased burdens on teaching staff in terms of the time commitment needed to develop or localize materials (at least initially). Enthusiastic students bring their own burdens for teaching staff who find that they then have to deal with increased communications (email, discussion forum inputs and monitoring, and so on) and greater demands for learning support.

Key to a successful integration, therefore, is a careful marshalling of the teachers' own motivation to enhance the learning of their students; in tandem with supporting structures and resources that allow innovation in practice without overwhelming overheads in time commitment and preparation.

BOOM AND BUST

Many forays into e-Learning across the world have been expensive failures: high costs combined with high dropout rates and littered with the casualties of over-stretched 'killer applications' that never really made it. The design and delivery of e-Learning in the future will therefore be decisive. However, there is always the risk that other almost symbiotic aspects of the educational computing phenomenon may contrive to make even the most useful and effective examples of e-Learning a failure. Innovation will be unlikely to survive the onslaught of problems that can arise in the underlying computing infrastructure, the level of technical support, the technical competence of teachers and students, the ease of access to the technology and its costs. Boom and bust, then, is always going to be a potential feature of e-Learning development.

e-business, like e-Learning, is an example of the integration of technology in our everyday lives which is increasing massively year on year but which has had at least one major cycle of boom and bust. Buying online makes perfect sense, no more long waits at checkout counters, no more high profit mark-ups to retail outlets. In the early 1990s investment was high and dot.com companies were all the rage, but by 2000 the dot.com revolution had virtually collapsed and was being labelled the dot.bomb. But in 2005 the tide seems to have turned and *The Economist* business magazine was reporting that dot.coms are back and are approaching the levels of viability that were first projected.

The history of educational computing has also had its comparatively less visible booms and busts but all the signs are that it too, in the form of e-Learning, is beginning to surge forward on a solid new platform of usability and effectiveness. It certainly presents challenges for the education sector. Without investment in institutional and national infrastructure, and without concerted efforts to ensure that educators can see 'what's in it for them', staff and students may be left insufficiently motivated to explore the innovations that e-Learning offers. How much of this will become easier over time with falling prices of technology and an increasingly technology-aware population remains to be seen. However, with the quality and diversity of product and process in e-Learning as it is today, there is every reason to be optimistic!

3 A Potted History of e-Learning

WHERE HAS e-LEARNING COME FROM?

New as it may be, at least in the form we have known it over the past 10–15 years, online learning actually has a long and sometimes distinguished history. We say 'sometimes distinguished' because some aspects of the developments have been more by accident than design! The story begins in the 1920s with Sydney Pressey's testing machine. Designed primarily for testing it quickly became associated with teaching, although its use as a teaching machine was perhaps something of an afterthought, as the title of the launching paper illustrates: 'A simple apparatus that gives tests and scores – and teaches' (Pressey, 1926). The approach based on this work became known as 'programmed instruction' or 'programmed learning', with the sequence of learning and assessment activities arranged in a linear fashion for the individual learner. The learner progresses from one section to the next by demonstrating they have learned the material in the previous section. According to the University of Houston's A Hypertext History of Instructional Design website (UH, 2005), Pressey took his inspiration for programmed learning from Edward Thorndike's earlier (1912: 165) observation: 'If, by a miracle of mechanical ingenuity, a book could be so arranged that only to him who had done what was directed on page one would page two become visible, and so on, much that now requires personal instruction could be managed by print'.

> ### 🖰 Box 3.1
>
> Explore the history of teaching machines and the simplicity of Pressey's early approaches at the University of Houston's A Hypertext History of Instructional Design website (http://www.coe.uh.edu/courses/cuin6373/idhistory/Pressey). Hardly Thorndike's 'miracle of mechanical ingenuity' but quite revolutionary in the 1920s.

To this day, 'programmed learning' printed texts are widely available as examination revision aids and similar 'drill and practice' resources. However, it was Pressey that first took the step of committing the task to machines. In time, more sophisticated branching sequences, allowing different pathways to be followed according to the learner's answers or indeed study needs (see Crowder, 1960), and complex matrix response systems with interdependent networked pathways were introduced to programmed learning systems (see Egan, 1974). The basic learning activities in all these variants automatically invoke assessment routines that greet success with some form of reward – screen congratulations perhaps or exemption from further similar questions. Failure is invariably met with some form of remedial activity, for example, an instruction to repeat the task or to undertake some revision.

Programmed instruction or learning became the mainstay of the Behaviourist movement in education, a model that sees repetition and reward/sanction based feedback as key determinants in helping a learner to assimilate new learning. The main champion of this success–move on/failure–repeat (or success–reward/failure–sanction) model of learning was Burrhus Frederic Skinner, a Harvard psychologist, more usually known as B.F. Skinner. He took up programmed instruction ideas enthusiastically, focusing his research interests on exploring what types of stimulation could support learning and how behaviour could be influenced through providing feedback. Technology seemed the obvious answer for providing individual feedback to students. In 1958, he built a teaching machine, the 'Skinner box', which facilitated his experimental observations. These invariably involved an exploration of 'operant conditioning' where immediate feedback was given to students who undertook programmed instruction. The students were given clear and concise instructions in relation to the chosen (behavioural) learning objectives and were allowed to pace themselves when working through them. Such was his belief in the power of programmed instruction that he remained a champion of the approach through to his death in 1990.

🖱 **Box 3.2**

Check out the Skinner Foundation at http://www.bfskinner.org/. How do you feel about this approach to learning through computers? Can you identify a good purpose for programmed instruction in your learning context?

Skinner argued strongly that 'properly programmed instruction is never drill if that means going over material again and again until it is learned' (1984: 951), but in truth, most programmed instruction is unsophisticated and is often described as 'drill and practice'. In essence, the computer in this mode simply provides tutorial material and then tests the learner by means of a series of questions on knowledge that they have been expected to assimilate. The ethos is entirely content centred with little attention to the learners and the variety of their learning styles or needs. However, even Seymour Papert, the champion of novel uses of computers in education such as Logo, would not rule it out completely as part of the educational repertoire: 'Drill and practice might be a good thing. There are some statistics to show that drill and practice will produce some significant improvement in standardized achievement scores, and I don't want to deny that' (1984: 26). Within the same quote, however, Papert set out what has come to be the 'party line' on learning with computers:

> But if we think of computers in terms of five or ten years from now, is drill and practice going to be a typical use? I think not. Giving to children microworlds that have – whether through Logo, or wordprocessing, or access to the computer in a more creative way – a more child-centred, free flowing, intuitive approach, that style of using the computer is what we need to learn about now, because that is what the future needs. (1984: 26)

> #### 🖱 Box 3.3
>
> Take your own position on drill and practice by visiting a site that actively promotes its benefits. For example, search out some of the drill and practice software sites listed by the Saskatoon Public School Division in Canada. http://olc.spsd.sk.ca/DE/PD/instr/strats/drill/index. html. On the front page of the site, the Saskatoon school board argues that good drill and practice software 'provides feedback to students, explains how to get the correct answer, and contains a management system to keep track of student progress'. What do you think?

From its mechanical beginnings in Pressey's 1920s experimental machine, educational technology had to wait over 40 years before a rapid growth in machine-based learning developments began in earnest. One of the most important stimuli of the new thinking was Marshall McLuhan's 1964 book *Understanding Media: The Extensions of Man*. McLuhan, a Canadian sociologist who coined the phrase 'the medium is the message', initiated a debate that has continued to rage until the present day, with little prospect of it dissipating. The essence of his work was to draw attention to the impact which 'electric' media, and in particular the television, was having on contemporary society. In 1966, Patrick Suppes, a Stanford University educationalist, was predicting that 'in a few more years, millions of school children will have access to … the personal services of a tutor as well informed and responsive as Aristotle' (1966: 207). While the actual usefulness of having Aristotle as a source of knowledge might be challenged today, the sentiment is clearly resonant with the expertise now available to learners through the World Wide Web.

In 1970, Alvin Tofler used the phrase 'future shock' to describe the effect on individuals and society, of the 'disease' of too much change in too little time. His book of the same name created a huge stir with its basic contention that society was not ready for the major social and technological changes that he argued were inevitable in the future. He questioned the outlook for school-based education and, with an inkling of the World Wide Web to come, predicted that the student of the future would have, at home, 'vast libraries of data available to him via computerized information retrieval systems' (1970: 244). However, it is possible that his urging the world to action was dissipated by some of his less realistic predictions, for example: 'Even now we should be training cadres of young people for life in submarine communities' (1970: 365).

In his 1979 book, *The Mighty Micro*, Christopher Evans, a British psychologist and computer scientist, took his focus on the future from the microcomputer revolution. This had begun two years earlier with the launch of the first production-line micros from Tandy, Apple and Commodore. He envisaged a world of 'cheap, universal computer power … [which would] … result in a gradual loosening of restraints on the movement of information within a society. The world of the 1980s and 1990s will be dominated not only by cheap electronic data processing, but also by virtually infinite electronic data transmission' (1979: 208). He predicted that the future ease and freedom of the electronic communication of information would, for example, precipitate the collapse of the Soviet Union and would lead to a shift from school-based education to computer-based education in the home. While somewhat exaggerated in his claims, perhaps, the general importance of the information revolution is captured in his predictions.

Another prominent futurologist around this time was Tom Stonier, a professor of science and society at the University of Bradford. His views were eventually to appear in his book, *The Wealth of Information* (Stonier, 1983) in which he argued passionately that the ability to access and use information was the key to the future wealth of any nation and its citizens. On the basis that an 'educated workforce learns how to exploit technology; an ignorant one becomes its victim' (1983: 39) he insisted that information technology and education must be harnessed together. He also echoed the previous writers' projections of the imminent rise of home-based education, predicting that the home centre 'tied via telephones, airwaves, or local cable television to local education authorities, … to national and international computer network systems … and … to global library archives … will have information available which vastly exceeds the largest city library' (pp. 172–3). Again, this is not far off being a vision of the Internet and World Wide Web today.

HOW DID WE GET TO WHERE WE ARE?

With the predictions in the background, it is worth taking a brief look at the actions and developments that actually occurred during the second half of the last century, starting with the 1960s.

The 1960s

It can be argued that most of the more positive roles for computers in education were first articulated during the 1960s. The substantial proceedings from the 1965 annual conference of the American Federation of Information Processing Societies, which took as its focus the potential for computers in education, was particularly important. Ralph Gerard, first dean of the Graduate Division in the newly formed University of California, Irvine summed up his address to the conference on computers in education with the comment: 'of the many opportunities [afforded by computers] for aiding man to handle himself collectively, in my judgement, the improved teaching of the young, to be effective members in society, is the greatest of all' (1967: xxi).

The period is littered with milestone events that set the scene for later policy-making. The following time line lists some of the important events in the UK:

- 1963: The British Computer Society establishes its Schools' Committee to promote computer studies in schools.
- 1965: The first computer is installed in a UK school.
- 1967: The National Council for Educational Technology (NCET) is established.
- 1967: The Universities' Grants Committee and the Computer Board set up a working party to review the requirements for computer use in universities.
- 1969: The National Council for Educational Technology releases three reports focusing on computers in education (NCET, 1969a; 1969b, 1969c).
- 1969: The Scottish Office releases its interim Computers in Schools report (the Bellis Report, 1969, with the final report appearing in 1972).

One of the 1969 National Council for Educational Technology reports, 'Computer based learning systems: a programme for research and development' (NCET, 1969c) is particularly interesting for offering one of the first authoritative outlines of the role for computers in simulation, modelling, problem-solving and information storage in education (albeit with a bias towards higher education and training). The working party considered that 'the computer has great potential ... [to extend] the student's experience beyond the bounds usually set by current educational techniques' (p. 22), for example in:

- solving problems in medical diagnosis;
- illuminating principles, and enabling their application, in situations outside the student's usual experience;
- using rapid data analysis for testing and formulating hypotheses;
- simulating complex situations which would be too expensive, too time-consuming or impossible to provide otherwise;
- storing information for student usage;
- educating students about computing per se.

They did not confine themselves to this, however, and used analyses from organizations such as the RAND Corporation to predict that computer-managed learning would become more widespread in education and training. They predicted that by 1992 facsimile newspapers and magazines would be printed at home. Furthermore

> small specialized information-retrieval units ... will become standard library equipment by about 1975 ... [these units being] modified TV sets connected via a multiplexer to exchangeable magnetic-disk files of enormous capacity. Control will be viewer-exercised by cheap pointing devices ... or by orthogo-nal-potentiometer devices, such as the SRI 'mouse'. (NCET, 1969c: 81–2)

🖱 Box 3.4

Find out about computer-managed learning systems. One of the oldest is Plato (see http://www.plato.com), while more recent developments have sometimes been called 'integrated learning systems'. These include the SuccessMaker Enterprise system at http://www.rm.com and CompassLearning's Odyssey system (view the demo on http://www.compasslearning.com/). What type of learning approach do these systems use?

The National Council for Educational Technology also warned of cultural problems that would be experienced as a result of most of the high-quality computer-based materials being from North America, but they baulked at one task in their future-gazing. They declined to estimate the costs of introducing computers into education, though they did make a stab at a benefit-to-cost ratio, proposing that it could be calculated thus (NCET, 1969c: 66):

$$({}^B\!/_C)_{CAI} = \{{}^1\!/_r(0.047)p^2({}^{dh}\!/_h)g_0\}/_{\text{(Discounted Costs of Implementing CAI)}}$$

There has never been any indication that the formula was ever followed up!

The 1970s

The 1970s were not short of milestones either. The Palo Alto Research Center (PARC) was founded by the Xerox Corporation in 1970 and has played a major role to the present day in designing and developing innovative technologies. One of the early ventures was Alan Kay's Dynabook, which was conceptualized as a portable, rugged computer with high-resolution graphic displays that would allow children to explore worlds of their own making. The team developed the graphical user interface and mouse, considered more appropriate for children than a keyboard and text commands (Kay and Goldberg, 1977). Smalltalk, the first object-oriented programming language, was designed for the Dynabook, specifically for young students to compose ideas without needing to master complex programming (Roschelle et al., 1998). These early developments led to the Macintosh and the graphical user interfaces used in various devices today.

The importance of computing for society was given a powerful endorsement by the Carnegie Commission in 1972, liking computing to the written word, the printing press and universal public education as the fourth major revolution in education. In the same year, in the UK the 1969 National Council for Educational Technology recommendations for a computer-assisted learning initiative were finally approved by the then Secretary of State for Education and Science, Margaret Thatcher. The first large-scale UK development project, the four-year National Development Programme for Computer Based Learning (NDPCAL) commenced in 1973 and was eventually to establish centres of excellence in computer-based learning at a number of universities. The NDPCAL activities, as they progressed from 1973 to 1977, were restricted to large mainframe computers, even though the first kit-form microcomputer (the ALTAIR) had actually been released in the USA in 1974. Despite the domination of programmed learning at the time, the programme's director, Richard Hooper, was in no doubt as to how computers could contribute to education more generally. In his words it should 'also provide the learner with a 'laboratory' … to model and try out theories, to practise skills, to see what would happen if certain variables of a given model are changed, to analyse data' (1975: 14).

In 1976, while educational technology developments were gathering pace, the then UK Prime Minister, James Callaghan, made his famous Ruskin speech in which he bluntly told schools that they should do more to give young people the skills necessary for the workplace. A year later, just as NDPCAL was finishing, the technology of business and manufacture, and indeed of education, was turned on its head with the arrival of the first microcomputers from Tandy, Commodore and Apple. In 1978 the BBC Horizon television programme, *Now the Chips Are Down*, questioned Britain's readiness to embrace the problems and opportunities that the microelectronic revolution would inevitably bring. With its stinging last words 'The silence is terrifying', directed at government inaction, the programme is widely considered to have galvanized the government into initiating microelectronics awareness programmes for industry, commerce, universities and schools. One year later Christopher Evans was adding to the pressure:

> Human beings just do not have a conceptual experience of the exponential. In our brief life-span we normally experience only linear change … The point is important, for computer technology is embarking on a period of exponential growth and social and economic changes will probably occur in its wake … at the same conceptually unmanageable pace. (Evans, 1979: 102)

The 1980s and 1990s

As Evans predicted, the 1980s were indeed characterized by an unprecedented interest in all aspects of educational computing and an equally unprecedented growth in its applications. Between 1980 and 1986, the UK government provided computers for schools (through the Department of Industry's Micros in Schools schemes) and attempted to address the huge educational software and training needs, through the Department of Education and Science's Microelectronics Education Programme (MEP). The MEP sponsored developments initially in four areas: computer-based learning, communications and information systems, electronic and control technology (essentially robotics and electronic remote control systems) and computer studies. In its later stages a fifth area, primary education, was added; a sign of the commitment of policy-makers to 'start early' in integrating computing in education. Educationalists began to take up a variety of entrenched positions from which to lobby, forcefully in many cases, for their own views on how education should respond to the information technology future. The academic lobby promoted the study of the computer per se (for example, programming and hardware) while the vocational lobby promoted the learning of computing skills for particular jobs (for example, spreadsheets for accountants and wordprocessors for secretaries). Another group, the life-skills lobby, promoted computer literacy, for example learning to cope with electronic information systems in an increasingly computerized society. Yet another group, the educational lobby, promoted the computer as a vehicle for learning, for example learning with the help of integrated learning systems such as those in Box 3.3, CD-ROM encyclopedias and Logo 'microworlds'.

🖱 Box 3.5

See what you can find out about Logo 'microworlds' (for example, try some of the demos of microworlds at the Logo Computer Systems Inc site: http://www.microworlds.com/). How would such a learning environment fit your needs?

If you have explored microworld-type sites in Box 3.5, you may have concluded that they represent very different aspects of e-Learning than those in Box 3.4. And we would agree with you. The former is a 'constructivist' learning environment, in which learners create their own learning and knowledge, while the latter is a sophisticated teaching system in which the knowledge is provided and the learners are tested on their progress in learning it. However, you will probably have noticed that the learning environment based on Logo (or similar systems), is in fact a very restricted one in which a specialized language needs to be learned for the students to create their learning activities.

Box 3.6

In the case of microworlds the language to be learned is Logo, and there are other variants of its use in a similar constructivist manner. See, for example, the Massachusetts Institute of Technology's 'Programmable Bricks' at http://www.media.mit.edu/groups/el/projects/legologo/ or the demos and tutorials at http://www.logosurvey.co.uk/).

There are also other languages, such as the logic-based ProLog, that provide a means of direct programming communication with the computer. In essence, these programming languages enable students to create their own learning environment and to solve problems, albeit usually highly contrived and somewhat esoteric. In theory, the skills of reasoning, analysing and hypothesis testing, and so on, and the eventual arrival at acceptable solutions, are argued to transfer to the more mundane contexts that everyday life throws up. For some educationalists this claim may be a bit of a stretch but the Logo environment particularly is one that retains strong educational advocacy across the globe.

The 'computer as teacher' is the essential concept for the managed or integrated learning systems of Box 3.4, offering the student a self-pacing, non-judgemental (at least in the human sense) and individualized learning environment. Some of these systems attempt to address higher-order skills, such as criticism in literature studies, but for the most part they are targeted at raising the basic literacy and numeracy skills of low achievers – particularly where there is a culture of low achievement, for example, in some inner-city schools.

The 'teaching' machine of today is the ubiquitous personal computer, whether as a vehicle for the types of learning environments above or those that can be constructed online on the Internet. But some, such as the researchers at the Sony Computer Science Lab in Tokyo (http://www.csl.

sony.co.jp/perspective_e.html), would urge us to think 'outside the box', to seek innovation that is not tied to personal computers. Since their inception in 1988, their research has centred on the area of HCI (the human–computer interface) and on the nature and type of devices and software that will in the future best allow learning in human-oriented environments. In exploring devices such as a 'wearable key', to enable access to a computer, and software such as GazeLink, which enables an inboard-camera to capture screen material from one machine and project it onto another machine, they promote values such as amusement and beauty in addition to the conventional standards of efficiency and usability. They argue that: 'Computers are convenient because they are dull: in pursuit of universal usability and productivity we adopted uniformity of interaction across applications and platforms. We as humans, however, prefer variety to uniformity' (Poupyrev et al., 2002).

While such developments will continue to push the boundaries of interaction, the most important development in the field of educational computing in the 1990s was that of the Internet.

THE EMERGENCE OF THE INTERNET

Although educational software is popular in its own right, it is the interconnectivity supplied by the Internet, and the huge resources made available through the World Wide Web, that are the primary underpinnings of e-Learning. Skinner had a vision of teaching machines but others, like the futurologists above, had a vision of huge stores of knowledge being accessible at the press of a button, stores of knowledge that would provide a learning environment in their own right for future generations of learners. One such was Vannevar Bush, who was director of the US Office of Scientific Research and Development in 1945 when he contributed an article entitled 'As we may think' to the *Atlantic Monthly*. The editor prefaced the paper with the comment: 'Now, says Dr Bush, instruments are at hand which, if properly developed, will give man access to and command over the inherited knowledge of the ages.' And in the article, Bush went on to review the many developments then happening before challenging the reader to:

> Consider a future device for individual use, which is a sort of mechanized private file and library. It needs a name, and, to coin one at random, 'memex' will do. A memex is a device in which an individual stores all his books, records, and communications, and which is mechanized so that it may be

consulted with exceeding speed and flexibility. It is an enlarged intimate supplement to his memory. It consists of a desk ... [O]n the top are slanting translucent screens, on which material can be projected for convenient reading. There is a keyboard, and sets of buttons and levers. (Bush, 1945)

Bush's desk is not quite the iPod, Blackberry or memory stick of today but his prescience was remarkable. Various developments were sparked off in the post-war period but it was not until 1969 that the US government began to lay the foundations of a world wide resource for individuals to tap into using personal computers. The innovation they commissioned was the world's first linked network of computers (between the universities: Stanford, University of California, Santa Barbara, University of California at Los Angeles and Utah). Called the Advanced Research Projects Agency Network (ARPANET), it went live in 1969 and both stimulated the growth of email and became the major precursor of today's Internet. The idea of sharing mainframe computers emerged during the cold war to avoid annihilation of computing resources in the event of an 'electrical' strike on the USA. The idea was to link each machine to each other machine rather than each to a central machine only. If any one machine in one area was knocked out, so the theory went, messages could still get through!

In 1969, the first email on the ARPANET was sent, testing to see if the process worked (check out an image of the actual journal entry, which was made on the occasion, at http://en.wikipedia.org/wiki/Image:First-arpanet-imp-log.jpg). Then in 1971 Ray Tomlinson was the first to use the '@' notation in user IDs. Today email has taken off in a manner that Tomlinson could not have dreamt. IDC, the information technology and telecommunications industry analysts, for example, estimate that in 2006 more than 60 billion emails will be sent every day; up from 31 billion in 2003. But it is another feature of the Internet, the World Wide Web as it is known, that has really enabled e-Learning on a colossal scale.

In 1990, Tim Berners-Lee (then a research fellow at CERN, the European Laboratory for Particle Physics, but now Sir Tim Berners-Lee!), argued the need for a way to be found to link information systems. And he proposed a way to do it using a hypertext system. He had a vision of a global hypertext database supported by the Internet. He launched the first website that same year based on his pioneering work, which had led to the integration of hypertext and the Internet and the three underpinning standards: the universal resource locator (URL), the HyperText Markup Language (HTML) and the HyperText Transfer Protocol (HTTP). At the time that he wrote the first browser editor in 1990, few people appreciated the potential but within a very few years the World Wide Web that he had initiated was a worldwide phenomenon. In July 1997, for example, the broadcast of images taken by Pathfinder on Mars is reported to have generated 46 million hits in one day on the National Aeronautics and Space Administration (NASA) website (http://www.factmonster.com/ipka/A0193167.html). The volume of educational resources now available through the Web is quite staggering. Just two educational sites will illustrate the magnitude of Berners-Lee's envisioned Web of linked information systems. With some 142 million objects in their collections, the 18 museums of the Smithsonian Institution are accessible at http://www.si.edu/, while the US government funded Education Resources Information Centre (ERIC) provides access to the million items of educational resources (research report, teaching guides, books, and so on) it holds at http://www.eric.ed.gov.

🖰 Box 3.7

Check out Tim Berners-Lee's actual proposal to CERN to create the hypertext-linked system we know today as the World Wide Web. It can be found at http://www.3.org/History/1989/proposal.html. The first website created by him is also available at http://www.3.org/History/19921103-hypertext/hypertext/WWW/TheProject.html. Find out more details on the history of the Web and join like-minded user groups including those on the Living Internet website. This site provides an overview of the Web including its history and design, and key features such as email and MUDs and so on. Check out its unusual table of contents designed within and for the Internet on its front page at http://www.livingInternet.com/

The Computer History museum is also a fun place for a rainy afternoon! Here you can trace the myths and legends in an informal tongue-in-cheek style. For example, as Danny Cohen writes: 'In the Beginning, ARPA created the ARPANET. And the ARPANET was without form and void.' http://www.computerhistory.org/exhibits/Internet_history/

🖱 **Box 3.8**

You can emulate the experiences of early Web environments on another very interesting site: the Déjà vu site – Pages from Those Days at http://www.dejavu.org. Try it out!

To discuss 'all things Internet' a bit more seriously, why not join the '.net' magazine forum http://forum.netmag.co.uk/ or join one of the many long-running scholarly user groups dedicated to studying and developing the Internet, such as H-NET (the Humanities and Social Sciences Online website) at http://www.h-net.msu.edu/. The H-NET site publishes peer-reviewed essays, multimedia materials and discussions about the Internet from a humanities/social sciences perspective.

Table 3.1   Learning tools and environments for online learning

Tools	Environments
Tools for working with information: • browsers to access the online resources • search engines to 'query' the various databases and repositories of information	Content-focused environments: • online integrated or learning management systems • repositories of learning materials (lesson plans, case studies, and so on)
Tools for interaction: • email, bulletin boards and discussion forums, chat facilities • accessibility tools for the physically disadvantaged	Learner-centred environments: • virtual learning environments • multi-user object-oriented systems (MOOs) • a 'Communal Yottaspace' of knowledge

Apart from burgeoning hugely in size and in the number of its users, the Web has not changed much since Berners-Lee's original version. However, there have been major developments in the Internet and Web-based tools and environments available to learners. Table 3.1, sets out a simplified breakdown of the types of these tools and environments.

The prospect of learners being able to access and, most importantly, contribute communally to an almost unimaginably vast range of knowledge is set to revolutionize education, and we turn to this prospect next.

4 e-Learning – An Educational Revolution

This chapter develops the notion that new technologies have revolutionized our conception of knowledge – from something some people might have, to something which everyone should be able to find. The distinction has grown exponentially since the early days of the Internet. Before its inception, people relied on an education that was relatively fixed in its knowledge content, with the extensions into the wider knowledge realms being largely the preserve of experts. Computer-based learning in its various generations has acted to open up the world of knowledge to everyone and its most powerful variant, online e-Learning, has become a catalyst that has enabled huge changes in what is learned and who is able to learn it. It is essential for the economic prosperity of the individual and society, and for the social cohesion that sustains it, to have the facility to acquire knowledge when it is needed and in a form that meets the purpose for which it was sought. Society has a duty to invest in improving access to education and knowledge for all citizens and, as a result, education systems are evolving to cope with or exploit massive changes in a number of key areas including:

- access to more knowledge than ever before;
- new learning skills for the twenty-first century;
- the maximizing of learning opportunities through e-Learning;
- the emergence of a society of lifelong learners;
- a recognition of the interests and needs of the 'Internet generation';

- the implications of globalization for cultural diversity;
- greater inclusivity in education through e-Learning;
- the removal of time and location limitations.

We now look at these issues in turn.

ACCESS TO MORE KNOWLEDGE THAN EVER BEFORE

Increasingly powerful computers, combined with the development of the World Wide Web, have meant that much more information is much more accessible than ever before. Indeed, it is at our very fingertips as the personal computer acts as a portal to the connected world. e-Learning has the potential to offer, at any time and place, richer resources than most traditional methods of delivering learning and teaching. For example, consider the collection of resources available to students available in any museum. The local students who can physically and conveniently visit the museum will no doubt appreciate the opportunity to have primary sources for intimate study but for the large number of other students who may need to access the museum, physical distance may be only one of many problems they face. Traditionally, schools would arrange a 'school visit' to the museum and the museum would in turn provide guided tours, work areas and perhaps some resources. Even then the likelihood is that it would only be schools that are relatively local. Apart from transport logistics, which automatically restrict the number of students, the museum itself would put constraints on the numbers it can handle at any one time owing to such issues as 'flow control' in the museum building and the lack of capacity for guides to communicate with other than relatively small groups. Now consider the emerging situation in which the collections of a wide range of museums around the world are beginning to be made available to the same students on their desktops. Not to take away from the undoubted excitement and value of a real visit, virtual access to museums presents a wealth of learning resources and opportunities only dreamt of a few decades ago. And not just for learners, such developments have the potential to impact significantly on the way lecturers incorporate access to the resources and design their courses to enable individual study and deeper reflection.

> **🖱 Box 4.1**
>
> Institutions with large collections of materials, such as the British Museum, are leading the way in exploring how online databases can deliver rich resources at any time and place. The Education Department of the British Museum has designed its site to offer students a range of learning experiences including videos, puzzles, study tasks and challenges as well as objects and buildings to explore. Check this out at http://www.thebritishmuseum.ac.uk/

At the forefront in this type of information dissemination are those initiatives that are involved in developing, collating and disseminating large collections of resources. The Scottish Cultural Resources across the Network (SCRAN at http://www.scran.ac.uk) is an example of such a digital collection of some 325,000 resource items, including video, artefacts and paintings from over 100 museums and other sources across Scotland. The increased ease of selection and dissemination of multimedia materials allows online resources to surpass, at least in quantity, local collections previously available to learners. Faster connections not only translate into more accessible materials but also allow access to a wider and richer content. As bandwidth increases, audio-video streaming and video-conferencing will create increasing opportunities for linking learners with experts in an online discourse that is supported by feedback and remote interactivity.

Access to collections of resources specifically designed for education is another important avenue leading to knowledge and knowledge creation, especially in locations in which access to public education is limited by remoteness or economic disadvantage. One example of this type of resource is the so-called Virtual Colombo Plan (details at http://www.ausaid.gov.au/keyaid/vcp.cfm), a major initiative sponsored by the World Bank and the Australian government. This is a comprehensive site offering a wide range of opportunities for scholarships, collaborations and major development initiatives for students and educationalists from Pacific Rim and South-East Asian countries. The site offers links through to learning resource providers such as AchieveOnline at http://www.achieveonline.

com.au/. Such sites allow offshore students from developing nations to participate in lectures at Australian universities via e-Learning across the Web, often by means of satellite-based video-conferencing.

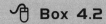 **Box 4.2**

Check out the Canadian-based Commonwealth of Learning (COL), which draws its membership from the 59 countries of the Common-wealth. The Commonwealth of Learning sees e-Learning and the electronic provision of resources to be one of its key weapons (along with collaboration, exchange, investment and capacity-building) in the struggle to educate the estimated 100 million children who have no access to schools in the member countries. It also offers training for the 15 million 'untrained or under trained' teachers that engage with them. Check out the site and its facilities at http://www. col.org/resources/.

Information available to students in an e-Learning environment goes beyond issues of ease of use and actually moves access and information into the student's domain. This is a fundamental change in the ownership of the information itself in the sense of it now being shared – a key step in personalized knowledge creation.

NEW LEARNING SKILLS FOR THE TWENTY-FIRST CENTURY

Knowledge, whether self-created from appropriate e-Learning resources or assimilated from ready-made learning materials, is vital for an individual's development, but perhaps more important is the use of e-Learning to assist in delivering the wider range of learning skills deemed necessary for modern times. As mentioned earlier, the US-based Partnership for 21st Century Skills has attempted to identify the set of skills needed to assist students in meeting the increasingly diverse demands from society and workplace (http://www.21stcenturyskills.org/). The Partnership argues for the development of three knowledge areas in every student: global awareness, civic literacy and financial, economic and business literacy. Two skills areas come under their focus:

- problem-solving, critical thinking and self-directional skills;
- information and communications technologies literacy.

The individual skill definitions for each of the two areas are detailed as follows:

Thinking, problem-solving, interpersonal and self-directional learning skills

- Critical thinking and systems thinking. Exercising sound reasoning in understanding and making complex choices, understanding the inter-connections among systems.
- Problem identification, formulation and solution. Ability to frame, analyse and solve problems.
- Creativity and intellectual curiosity. Developing, implementing and com-municating new ideas to others, staying open and responsive to new and diverse perspectives.
- Interpersonal and collaborative skills. Demonstrating teamwork and lead-ership; adapting to varied roles and responsibilities; working productively with others; exercising empathy; respecting diverse perspectives.
- Self-direction. Monitoring one's own understanding and learning needs, locating appropriate resources, transferring learning from one domain to another.
- Accountability and adaptability. Exercising personal responsibility and flexibility in personal, workplace and community contexts; setting and meeting high standards and goals for one's self and others; tolerating ambiguity.
- Social responsibility. Acting responsibly with the interests of the larger community in mind; demonstrating ethical behaviour in personal, work-place and community contexts.

Information and communication technology (ICT) Learning Skills

- Information and media literacy skills. Analysing, accessing, managing, integrating, evaluating and creating information in a variety of forms and media. Understanding the role of media in society.
- Communication skills. Understanding, managing and creating effective oral, written and multimedia communication in a variety of forms and contexts.
- Interpersonal and self-direction skills. Becoming more productive in accomplishing tasks and developing interest in improving own skills. (Partnership for 21st Century Skills, 2005)

Identifying and delivering key intellectual and technical skills is of interest to all educators. Nowhere are such skills more problematic to define than in the emerging field of e-Learning. Designing e-Learning courses, studying e-Learning environments, training e-Learning tutors and evaluating e-Learning outcomes all pose challenges. The rapid evolution of information and communications technology and its continued advancement will ensure that such challenges increase in complexity.

🖱 Box 4.3

Check out the US-based Jason Foundation for Education (http://www.jasonproject.org/) which is an example of a complex utilization of a variety of high technologies. Indeed it describes itself as a real-time source for real mathematics and science, offering real learning. The Foundation takes students on actual and virtual scientific expeditions that are designed to enthuse and engage them in both science and technology, and to provide professional development for teachers. Its interactive website offers video supplements and online broadcasts to places as diverse as the ground floor of the ocean, inside a volcano and even to Mars. Students can use a two-way satellite link to operate the JASON data collection vehicle remotely and they have a chance to use other 'real life' research tools such as global positioning systems (GPS), geographic information systems (GIS) and satellite remote sensing.

MAXIMIZING LEARNING OPPORTUNITIES THROUGH e-LEARNING

Most educationalists would agree that in today's education they have moved beyond the mere imparting of facts to the facilitating of the higher-order skills of creativity, problem-solving, analysis and evaluation. Students studying any subject will still have a quantum of facts and theories to assimilate but there will also be an increased imperative on them becoming immersed in the culture of the discipline. Donald (2002) argues that disciplines have different cultures and different ways of thinking and we would argue that helping students to learn to think like a physicist rather than to think about physics is a key aspiration for flexible, tailored e-Learning environments. Those who offer a type of apprenticeship, either cognitive or skills based, such as the medical colleges, have been the forerunners in developing approaches that immerse learners virtually in the discipline. Their curricula lend themselves to experimental instruction techniques such as a case-based research or simulations.

Disciplines where visual information forms a key component of learning, such as the fine arts, history and archaeology can also benefit significantly from enabling their students to access relevant materials on the Internet.

Box 4.4

We have presented a whistle-stop tour of software that assists learning but what about software that stops people from working (but not from learning!)? Check out satellite images of your neighbourhood by zooming into it using Google Earth at http://earth.google.com/. Then you might try all the places you have ever visited. It is guaranteed to stop geographers working for days!

Hyperlinking can be used to make connections between sources and thus supports understanding of key concepts and the cross-fertilization of ideas.

Box 4.5

Explore the highly hyperlinked resources of the Timeline of Art History at http://www.metmuseum.org/toah/splash.htm. This is a chronological, geographical and thematic exploration of the history of art from the collection of the Metropolitan Museum of Art in New York and includes additional maps, architectural sites, photography and links to relevant websites.

Where subjective interpretation is important, taking time to engage with materials and to examine a variety of different works at leisure is an integral part of knowledge acquisition. e-Learning provides students with such opportunities. The Perseus website, developed as a non-profit enterprise by Tufts University, embraces the concept of learning for all and provides access to primary sources, for example, full-text versions of nineteenth-century books and zoom-able maps of nineteenth-century London. The website's mission statement (see http://www.perseus.tufts.edu/) endorses the concept of access to learning materials for all and is worth setting out here:

> Perseus is an evolving digital library, engineering interactions through time, space and language. Our primary goal is to bring a wide range of source materials to as large an audience as possible. We anticipate that greater accessibility to the sources for the study of the humanities will strengthen the quality of questions, lead to new avenues of research and connect more people through the connection of ideas.

e-Learning environments can therefore assist students to interact with the objects of their study, which might not normally be available to them. Ancient manuscripts, for example, are too valuable to be studied physically and copies may be difficult to reproduce. When recognition of fine detail is important, online collections can support learners who wish to see the images enlarged. The accompanying annotations and links can be conveniently located in the e-Learning environment. A very important example of this, albeit in CD-ROM form only at present, is the digital version of the unique and priceless AD 800 *Book of Kells* (see http://www.bookofkells.ie). It contains the manuscript as well as features that allow the reader to explore the text and its intricate artwork in detail.

Learners can benefit from visual demonstrations of concepts or phenomena in a variety of science-related disciplines, such as mathematics, biochemistry, genetics and physics. Such visualization often holds the key to learners understanding the concepts that may be difficult for their tutors to explain and illustrate. e-Learning environments selected by the tutor or sought out by students can offer animations, models or simulations online, during lectures or wherever and whenever the students wish to go on the Web, to assist understanding and support connections between theory and practice. Conway's Game of Life (http://www.bitstorm.org/gameoflife/), for example, is a representation of emergent complexity or self-organizing systems. To study how elaborate patterns and behaviours can emerge from simple rules, students input their own patterns and study the results. It is interesting for biologists, mathematicians and economists, and indeed philosophers, among others, to observe the way that complex patterns can emerge from the implementation of very simple rules.

As academics become skilled in tailoring or creating environments, discipline-specific e-Learning environments will flourish. Many universities have recognized this and have made significant advances in using e-Learning to enhance their teaching. For one example, visit the links available on the Trinity College, Dublin, site (http://www.tcd.ie/CAPSL/clt/). These lead to project descriptions that give a sense of how e-Learning is impacting on disciplines as diverse as psychiatry and geography in this university.

Offering opportunities to create materials that transmit information and engage the learner in the culture of the discipline are key benefits of e-Learning environments but they are also a very powerful extension to 'cognitive apprenticeships' (Lajoie, 2000). In this mode, the e-Learning environment provides access to the thinking of experts, including in some instances direct interaction with them (asynchronously or synchronously). We will come back to cognitive apprenticeships in Chapter 6.

THE EMERGENCE OF A SOCIETY OF LIFELONG LEARNERS

For some decades now, lifelong learning as a concept and practice has been growing in importance as more people realize that they need continuously to develop their knowledge and skills in a rapidly changing world. According to the European Commission:

> Europe's future economy and society are being formed in the classrooms of today. Students need to be both well educated in their chosen field and digitally literate if they are to take part effectively in tomorrow's knowledge society. e-Learning – the integration of advanced information and communication technologies (ICT) into the education system – achieves both aims. Europe also needs to make learning a lifelong endeavour, with people of all ages continuously developing their skills. Here too, e-Learning can make a significant contribution, with both workers and organizations transforming the way they learn, interact and work. Moreover, e-Learning can promote social integration and

inclusion, opening access to learning for people with special needs and those living in difficult circumstances (marginalized groups, migrants, single parents, etc.). (eEurope, 2005)

The formal education system, which most people in the West have experienced, developed into its present form as a result of beliefs about learning and as an accommodation to various evolving economic, social and political conditions. Early schooling catered for elite sections of society and was designed to educate for a predestined leadership role. Learning was often conducted in one-to-one tutoring contexts or in relatively small groups of students led by a teacher. Some members of society were educated through apprenticeships provided either by trades guilds or by their parents as employers.

As nation-states in the West became interested in educating larger numbers of students, public state-run schools were formed and formal education systems were established. Schooling became compulsory for some age groups and the pressures of universal education meant that one-to-one tutoring and small-group learning did not transfer in any significant way to state schooling. It also meant the inception of forms of periodic assessment or grading as the standards of education being offered came under scrutiny. Currently, schoolchildren must conform to education systems that dictate when they attend school, the rate of delivery of material, the way in which it is delivered and the assessments made of their learning. In sacrificing flexibility in the structure of learning, however, society has arguably gained through increasing the flexibility of the outcomes of learning.

Properly implemented and supported, e-Learning approaches have the potential to overcome these traditional barriers to the way education is conceived and delivered. It can provide a resource-rich education for everyone, whether they come from the affluent suburbs, disadvantaged inner cities or isolated rural areas. New technologies call into question present models of educational delivery, including who the learners are, where and when they learn, what they are studying, how they are taught and assessed, and how much it costs in terms of teacher time and infrastructure. e-Learning is not without its major costs also, but its potential to reach all members of a society is very attractive, especially if existing costs for education do not bear up well under a value-for-money scrutiny.

Since its earliest beginnings, education has been traditionally designed to maintain the status quo, by focusing on teaching skills for a specific role usually determined by the status of the parents and the sex of the child.

Today education offers students an increasingly diverse array of options. Equality of opportunity has been both a product of and a driving force for the move from a role-based to ability-based society. The impact of new ways of learning calls for new structures for financing, governing and managing schools, as well as changing the nature of the way the state system operates. e-Learning is a central instrument in these changes.

Much can be learned not only by studying what is happening in other educational systems, but also in other areas of learning such as the workplace and the community. Once students leave school or university they have to continue to learn in their workplaces and communities, often reverting to older traditions of learning, namely, gaining knowledge through practical experience, one-on-one mentoring and formal apprenticeships. Models of learning that build on these highly communicative learning environments are facilitated by the forms of e-Learning that provide for interaction with peers and experts, for example through email, chat lines, wikis and blogs. The diversity of learning objectives, which online e-learning addresses, is driving the recognition that learning is not just for economic growth but is also an investment in human development.

THE INTERNET GENERATION

Today's young people are growing up as a part of the Internet generation and their ease with digital technology, and the access it gives them to almost unlimited opportunities for both broadly based and specialist learning, will undoubtedly result in them becoming a force for social transformation. We have seen the benign power of McLuhan's 'medium as message' with such transformations as the downturn in smoking, the concern for the environment and the reduction in developing nations' loan debts, all largely stimulated by mass information and education processes. This new generation, it is argued will not just create, think and learn differently, but will also act, work and even shop differently from previous generations. Don Tapscott, in his 1998 book, *Growing up Digital: The Rise of the Net Generation*, argues that schooling has remained modern, with its fixed notions of what must be learned and how it is to be learned, while lagging behind a society that has become postmodern. The prevailing learning model is constructivist, with 'reality' no longer an objective certainty but constructed by each of us in an interactive engagement with our environment and other people. It will be the unstoppable impact of the 'Net Generation' that will ultimately undermine any persisting absolutes in the education, government, business and community sectors of society and will cause everyone 'in authority' to re-evaluate their beliefs and activities.

> ### 🖱 Box 4.6
>
> Check out the website that Tapscott set up (http://www.growingupdigital.com/) to explore and expand on issues relating to the 'Net Generation'. He argues that the Net Generation will be the dominating force of the twenty-first century and that the new value system of the 'N-Gen' technology and way of life will differ greatly from today's. If you are already part of a 'cyber' community you can link to the website or you can add to or read excerpts from their database of viewer responses.

THE IMPLICATIONS OF GLOBALIZATION FOR CULTURAL IDENTITY

From the beginning when computers were first introduced in classrooms, and throughout the subsequent rapid developments of information and communications technology in education around the globe, questions have been raised about the relationship between culture and computers. The new technology brings people – individuals, communities and nations – closer together and creates better possibilities for collaboration and exchange of ideas and knowledge, but it also risks the loss of the richness and uniqueness of cultural identities. The underlying philosophy of e-Learning is about opening learning up to a wider variety of learners. However, it is clear that the cost of technology and access to the Internet is a barrier to access for learners in underdeveloped and impoverished nations. Mechanisms are needed to ensure that learners in these countries have access to e-Learning regardless of their or their nation's ability to pay for the infrastructural hardware and software. Easier said than done, no doubt, but network access does need to be extensive and cheap – if not free – to ensure e-Learning achieves its potential.

A more complex barrier to accessing to the potential of the Internet and e-Learning is the culture of any particular society or community. Technology is not neutral and the Internet comes to us with a very strong Western cultural bias. Cultures which espouse values different from those prevailing in the West, particularly the freedom of expression, whether political or otherwise, that is enshrined in most Western democracies, will resist universal access for all their citizens. Many such countries create their own websites and exercise their own firewalls, and today's Web does indeed reflect the language and social diversity of the modern world. The positive dimensions of self-growth, such as the creation of new technological applications, are to be applauded and may, according to the World Bank, be crucial to future development. In a recent report on closing the gap in education and technology the organization argues that a country's technological evolution follows three progressive stages: first, adoption of the technologies, then adaptation of the technologies to local needs and, finally, creation of new technologies themselves. The ultimate goal of lower-income countries, the report argues, should be to move towards the creation of new products and processes (de Ferranti et al., 2003). If countries are to create their own technologies and ways of incorporating them into their education, training and workplaces, then cultural considerations may be key to their future success or failure.

Nevertheless, e-Learning educators are continuing to consider how languages and cultures, particularly minority cultures, can be enriched and supported. The United National Educational, Scientific and Cultural Organization (UNESCO, 2001), for example, has expressed its concern both to protect and enhance cultural diversity worldwide, especially in the face of the increasingly global digital economy, and has deliberately set out to design its educational sector programmes to take this into account.

Clearly issues of cultural representation and identity are important in the global contexts of teaching across cultures and in addressing the digital divide that reflects the economic conditions across and within nations. However, it is also important to consider the same issues at a micro-level, that is, in the multicultural classroom. Many countries, especially in the European Union, which has an increasingly open border policy among member states, are facing an increase in students in their schools from cultures other than those indigenous to them. Like the USA and Canada, many

European nations have a long history of successful integration of successive waves of immigration and population movement, though some others, such as Ireland in the wake of its economic resurgence over the past decade or so, are experiencing the phenomenon of multicultural education as a relatively recent one. Part of the European e-Learning Programme, which runs until 2006, seeks to explore the effective use of information and communications technologies in both education and training as a contribution to social cohesion (Reding, 2002).

In Europe and North America, then, tutors in universities and teachers in many inner-city schools have truly multicultural communities of learners to accommodate, and experience would suggest that technology simply cannot be isolated from its social and environmental context. e-Learning designers and facilitators therefore need to take such factors as language competence, cultural background and learning style into account when creating and presenting the information and content for the e-Learning environments they provide. To help address the problems of diversity in the learner population, researchers have been interested in how different types of learners, often grouped by ethnicity, racial identity, linguistic differences and gender, interact with computers (for example, see Chisholm, 1996 and Turkle, 1994). The rose-tinted perception of the Internet and its e-Learning facilities being the great leveller of disadvantage, prejudice and social restriction must, however, be tempered by the reality of how difficult it is to surmount social division. Gorski (2001), for example, argues that even though women represented 50 per cent of the online population in the USA in the year 2000, they held only 7 per cent of all undergraduate engineering degrees and comprised only 20 per cent of all information technology professionals.

Many early studies which have examined the cultural aspects of educational technology in multicultural classrooms have suggested that the use of computers leads to positive changes, particularly for minority groups. For example, using computers in the classroom might be argued to foster an informal environment, allowing movement from the computer to other areas of the room and so complementing the kinaesthetic style of many African-American children (Jalali, 1989). Visual imagery, it was suggested, may be useful to some Native Americans who prefer to work with concrete images as way of understanding and remembering (More, 1989). Pairs and groups of three at the computers were also argued to match the preference for group problem-solving and personal interaction frequently exhibited by many Puerto Rican, Mexican-American and African-American children (Anderson, 1988). Not all minority groups, however, were found to have positive experiences working with the new technologies. According to More (1989), Native American children prefer private practice before public demonstration of learning and may avoid working on the computer if the computer monitor is visible to other students. Nevertheless, the earlier optimism in the value of promoting cultural diversity through communication technologies seems to have been justified. The United States Agency for International Development (USAID), for example, the long-established overseas development arm of the US government, places e-Learning approaches at the centre of its education. Their position reflects the aspirations of many national systems by:

- Supporting teacher professional development through computer-mediated networks that facilitate tele-collaboration;
- Developing networks that promote student collaboration both within their country and with students abroad
- Using technology to break down entrenched rote-based teaching practices and to support educational reform towards more student-centred learning;
- Using computers in classrooms for online access to the latest textbooks and teaching materials. (USAID, 2006)

However, there is a persistent concern about the impact on cultural diversity of the increasing globalization of the English language. This has been accelerated by the trends in interface and software developments, which have evolved from English-speaking 'office' cultures. Of the estimated 801.4 million Internet users in September 2004, the statistics on language confirm English as the dominant language but show that other languages make up a majority that is almost double the size of English usage. Table 4.1 sets out the figures.

The Enlace Quiché project in Guatemala is one of the USAID projects which is seeking to strengthen indigenous culture. It uses e-Learning approaches to prepare teachers in the Quiché region of Guatemala to teach in up to five of the local languages including K'iche and Ixil. Early results suggest it has been successful in blending the old Mayan cultures and the new technologies.

Table 4.1   Online language statistics for September 2001

Language	%	Language	%
English	35.2	Korean	3.9
Chinese	13.7	Italian	3.8
Spanish	9.0	Portuguese	3.1
Japanese	8.4	Dutch	1.7
German	6.9	Other	10.1
French	4.2		

Total users 801.4 million.

Source: Global Reach, 2005.

Box 4.7

Have a look at the Enlace Quiché website (http://www.enlace-quiche.org.gt/) to get a flavour of how e-Learning is being used to preserve and support indigenous languages and cultures. If you cannot speak Spanish, take a moment to reflect on how difficult it is for you to learn from a site that is not presented in your language, and therefore how difficult it might be for Guatemala's native Mayan students, 40 per cent of whom are not reckoned to have working knowledge of Spanish! To help yourself, though, go to http://www.babelfish.altavista.com and get a very serviceable translation into English for the site.

INCLUSIVE EDUCATION THROUGH ε-LEARNING

Advances in new technologies are making it easier to meet the needs of individual learners. Not only can learning environments be structured so that the learners can set the pace of their learning and control the delivery of information but, increasingly, e-Learning is able to cater for the individual learning styles of the students. However, there is still much work to be done before e-Learning is comprehensively a personalized concept. Research in this field in the UK has been concerned primarily with identifying problem situations and promoting equal access to computers.

Ever since the launch of the National Curriculum (DES, 1988) successive governments in the four UK countries (England, Wales, Northern Ireland and Scotland) have been committed to ensuring equal access for all students, regardless of location, age, first language, race, gender or disability, to technology in the classroom; both as an area of learning and skills development and as a means through which learning is facilitated (that is, e-Learning) (see, for example, NC, 2006a; 2006b).

If a society is committed to social inclusion, access to knowledge and knowledge creation should be embraced to the fullest possible extent. As we have argued earlier, e-Learning provides the opportunity to address the needs of a wider range of learners than ever before. e-Learning environments can, for example, meet the needs of school phobics, those in hospitals or restricted to home through illness or disability, second-chance learners and those who have moved to other countries and who wish to continue in their previous educational systems. They permit students in small, rural or low-income school districts, or who are in schools with only a few students interested in a specific topic, to take specialized courses that would ordinarily not be available to them. A rise in the numbers of those attending university, especially in countries where there is limited infrastructure such as China, India and Mexico, is stimulating global partnerships in distance learning through e-Learning environments created in more affluent or developed nations.

The UK's Ultralab research group has undertaken to address the needs of teenagers who find themselves outside traditional learning through the Notschool project (http://www.notschool.net) with

> none of the systemic barriers to learning which exist in traditional school environments, so that the process of reengagement in learning can be enabled. We remove all the rhetoric, strictures and structure of school including the need to meet face-to-face with a tutor or teacher. The key engagement is participation in an online learning community which is both asynchronous and distributed. (NESTA, 2005: 18)

Gender

The influence of gender on technology uptake and use is a widely studied issue and any discussion here can only cover a very small part of the overall debate. Initially, computers were seen as a primarily male reserve. Early research on technology and learning looked at the potential impact upon women, which Kramarae (1988) argued was for the most part ignored in the late 1980s. Benston (1988) believed that technist thinking equated to 'the right to control the world view' and described it as a 'male norm'. In opposition to this view, she argued, are the feminists who question whether this kind of domination over nature is legitimate. Turkle (1984) identified two general styles of computer mastery in her study of gender in US classrooms in the early 1980s. The 'hard approach' she believed was characteristic of students who are concerned with mastering the technology itself and who develop an orderly, rational and systematic approach to achieving defined goals. The 'soft approach' is more like that of an artist, and here learners often work by trial and error. Turkle's research findings suggest that hard and soft approaches are gender linked; hard associated with males and soft with females.

Not surprisingly, then, the number of women coming through to technology-related university courses is in decline. Carter and Jenkins (2001), for example, have reported that in the 1980s some 35 per cent of applicants for computer science degrees at UK universities were female, but had dropped to nearer 10 per cent by 2001. Newton and Beck have argued that the low number of women entering computer science is due to the fact that they are 'systematically discouraged from applying for courses in computing by their previous experience of computers and their perceptions of computing as a career' (1993: 131). This trend has continued through to today and at a recent conference for academics hosted by Microsoft and addressed by Bill Gates (Fried, 2005), Princeton University's engineering school dean, Maria Klawe, argued that the information Technology (IT) industry was simply not attractive to women. Perhaps a little tongue in cheek, she is reported to have said that she:

> is convinced more is needed, ideally something from Hollywood that glamorizes computer work in the same way that the popularity of law and medicine have helped draw more women to those fields. Just 15 percent of doctoral computer science students are women. At the top research schools, about the same number of undergraduate computer science students are women ... Klawe said that at this point her best hope is that Harry Potter's friend Hermione Granger decides to pursue a career in computer science. [Bill] Gates added that it is clear the industry is losing talented girls and women at many stages of their academic career, and that there probably is no single solution. 'I don't know the magic answer,' Gates said. (Fried, 2005)

The gender-related digital divide is a complex phenomenon. According to an Inter Press News agency report (Logan, 2005), for example, the gender gap has disappeared in some countries with high Internet penetration, such as Canada and the USA, but not in others such as Norway, Luxembourg and the UK. Also running counter to expectation, low penetration countries such as Mongolia, the Philippines and Thailand do not have a gender divide.

Generally speaking, there are significant differences in attitudes towards technology between girls and boys but access to a home computer will tend to give both boys and girls greater confidence, which then manifests itself in the classroom. In the main, girls tend to use computers as a tool (for example, for browsing the Web or word processing) more than boys who tend to engage more in entertainment and gaming aspects.

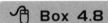 **Box 4.8**

AnimalWatch (at the University of Massachusetts Amherst's site http://ccbit.cs.umass.edu/ccbit/) is a mathematics tutor specifically designed to cater for the learning styles of girls using 'enhanced adaptive feedback'. The project has conducted evaluation studies with fifth grade US students and found that the program not only increases performance in mathematics but also decreases the standard deviation from the mean so that it is especially beneficial in targeting weak students. When you visit the website, why not click on the AnimalWatch adventures and either contribute a word problem or create an adventure?

In co-educational classrooms, there has long been a problem of ensuring equal access to the technology for girls in the face of more competitive, and even aggressive, modes of access-seeking displayed by boys. Without appropriate teacher control, boys tend to dominate the use of computers in the class. This is evident right through to university where open access facilities can be dominated by male students if some form of monitoring and equal access controls are not in place. When male students are not allowed to dominate, girls respond much more positively to computers. Even in single-sex circumstances, assertive girls do not display a domination mode of participation. Instead they work together without attempting to monopolize the work. However, boys in the same study marginalized their less able partners, proceeding to solve the problems themselves. Interacting online may impact on identity in different cultures. In a study on the Internet, Gender and Identity, for example, Japanese female students reported a change in who they felt they were when communicating online (Holmes et al., 1999).

Seniors

The digital divide is evident in that part of society we call the 'third age'. In the UK, for example, studies have shown that the percentage of adults using the Internet decreases with age, from 86 per cent for 16-to 24-year-olds to 12 per cent for over-65s (UK, 2001). For the most part, societies such as that which exists in the UK have accepted that senior management may not be as proficient in technology as junior members of staff. In less developed countries, however, the problem can be accentuated. If there is a strong cultural emphasis on respecting the elders and hierarchy of work relations, then pressure to use technology in the workplace can result in a shift of expertise from old to young and from senior to junior. This may result in serious tensions in the workplace. Older staff can easily become alienated by the new technology, as was found to be the case in the failure of the Accounts and Personnel Computerization Project of Ghana's Volta River Authority (Heeks, 2001).

Learners with special needs

The importance of e-Learning for communities of learners who experience access difficulties cannot be over-estimated as it offers a major avenue of learning opportunities for those who cannot avail themselves of the education provision most people would see as standard. The community of blind and partially sighted citizens provides a good example of important groups of people who can be inadvertently deprived of a quality education provision. For the estimated 7 million and 1 million visually impaired people in the European Union and the UK respectively, there are a number of ways in which e-Learning environments can be made maximally accessible. These include designing the online material and its delivery specifically for non-sighted or partially sighted users through the use of assistive technologies. To meet their need, websites are being designed for accessibility using such guidelines as the standards of the World Wide Web Consortium's Web Accessibility Initiative (WAI, at http://www.w3.org/WAI/). Assistive technologies such as voice recognition input (programmed using the Voice eXtensible Mark-up Language, VXML, at http://www.vxml.org/), interactive voice response (IVR) technology, screen-reading software (see, for example, JAWS for Windows at http://www.freedomscientific.com), screen magnifiers and Braille displays are also being increasingly used. In one example of collective action in Ireland, new ways of providing learning opportunities for visually impaired students are being pioneered by the Accessible Communities for E-Business (ACE) project (see http://www. inishnet.ie/).

There are many other groups of learners with special needs and circumstances that will prevent them from exploiting learning opportunities online. For example, a recent UK Improvement and Development Agency (IDeA) report (IDEA, 2005) quotes surveys suggesting that 72 per cent of unskilled workers have not used personal computers, mobile phones or digital televisions to access the Internet (Cabinet Office, 2004), 79 per cent of people receiving benefits lack basic practical information and communications technology skills (DfES, 2003) and 44 per cent of people who do not use the Internet see no reason or need to use it (ONS, 2005). Groups that suffer social exclusion, such as the homeless, single parents, people with health difficulties and people with learning difficulties, are unlikely to seek out the benefits of access to e-Learning and therefore present a challenge for the education system. One way to meet this challenge is to exploit the flexibility of e-Learning by using content that is tailored to their needs (including their literacy levels where relevant) and by taking the learning to where they are and when they want it. This is a community education strategy as opposed to school/college/university-based mainstream education strategies, and is being taken forward by local authorities, charitable organizations and so on.

All 'special' learners can now access a wealth of educational materials and resources from their homes and many also avail themselves of the mainstream facilities of such organizations as the UK's Open University (OU).

For example, there were 10,000 registered disabled people taking courses with the Open University in 2005 (http://www.open.ac.uk/about/ou/).

REMOVING TIME AND LOCATION LIMITATIONS

The choice of where and when to learn has traditionally been associated with flexible distance learning programmes offered by tertiary-level institutions such as the Open University mentioned above and there are strong indications that the numbers doing so are set to increase: 'The demand for high quality but inexpensive higher education seems likely to have a profound impact on universities over the next decade as the definition of higher education becomes uncertain' (OECD, 2000: 68).

The prospect of recruiting more students by providing greater choice is inevitably leading to increased competition between institutions both locally and internationally. Smaller institutions find themselves unable to compete with richer, well-known institutions, which can attract students in an increasingly global marketplace. As society experiments with how best to deliver compulsory education, similar issues are also raised in primary and secondary schools. One of the major developments in recent times has been the growth of education in the home. A small but significant proportion of parents in the US are seeking more personalized curricula for their children and are also growing increasingly concerned about the safety of state schools (*Washington Post*, 2000). The result is that the number of students being educated at home in the US more than tripled to 1.7 million in the period between 1990 and 2000. For educators in the home the Internet offers the benefits of choosing according to personal or family criteria from a huge range of resources and online courses.

The US-based Virtual High School offers a wide range of courses to schools both to enrich existing courses and to provide courses where there are gaps, for example when the school does not have the necessary teachers for a particular subject. However, since its programmes are presented entirely in an e-Learning environment, in this case based on the Blackboard system, it is also attractive to those who are being educated at home or who cannot easily travel to school owing to illness, for example. The breadth of curriculum offered is a major attraction also. For example, if students wish to take a course that is not offered in their own schools, a virtual school provision is a major attraction. Students are also able to proceed at their own pace. If they fail a course, they can repeat it without the indignity of having to join a class with younger students. The Virtual High School argues that online education, when designed and delivered with care and high expectations, can enhance communication between students and teachers, as well as among students. The online classroom can facilitate collaboration with peers around the world and students can engage with experts such as working scientists. In relation to those students with physical impairments, who may have difficulty attending conventional schools, the Virtual High School argues that online classrooms can encourage students to participate by reducing or removing any differences – perceived or real – arising from disability, social status, race or gender.

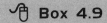 **Box 4.9**

Visit the Virtual High School site (at http://www.govhs.org/website.nsf) and try out a course demonstration.

Learning credits and the free movement of students

While the advantages of being able to choose where they are educated are clear for disadvantaged groups of students, a number of countries have been interested in creating an educational system in which all parents can choose where their children are educated. Several countries, including Australia, New Zealand, England, the USA and Chile, have experimented with the benefits of wider parental choice in the schooling of their children. Social and environmental (that is, primarily location) issues have introduced a degree of competition between schools and have prompted moves to create self-governing schools. Experiments on access to education by choice have included credit and voucher schemes, which represent the funds that the state would normally allocate for each student's education. These schemes are designed to enable students or their parents to choose any mix of schooling that suits their needs. In some cases this might mean the student taking 'a course here and a course there', chosen on the basis of perceived quality, cost or breadth of provision. In other cases credits might be 'spent' entirely with one education provider, for example, a creative arts training agency. Arguably many of the difficulties in choosing the right mix of education for any particular student access to education will be mitigated by the use of information and communications technologies to broaden access to a range of courses or other learning offerings. Such parental and student choice systems will inevitably increase the demand for online learning environments with the consequence that more 'virtual' school, university and training agency courses will emerge.

Wireless technologies

Optimal access to e-Learning requires that the delivery technology is available at any time, in a flexible manner throughout the learner's physical environment rather than in a fixed location such as a computer laboratory or classroom. But will the change happen overnight? No, for the most part new practice will exist alongside more traditional ways of working, in the same manner that people who get mobile phones do not immediately give up their landline. Instead, they may use the mobile initially for emergencies. Then, as they feel more comfortable with the technology, their use expands to calling friends and, ultimately, for long chats when stuck in traffic using their hands-free sets. Many universities have started wireless e-Learning in a similar manner by installing, for example, wireless facilities in fixed locations labs – despite the underlying idea of wireless being accessible anywhere. Arguably, placing a number of wireless-linked but locked down computers in a lab essentially undoes the benefits of wireless technology. However, once the students, tutors and so on get used to the technology, they often start to build on its use and within a short time accessing the learning resources may be moved into the park (weather permitting!). Some of the students will certainly prefer to choose where on campus they log in and, increasingly, a variety of educational institutions (universities, schools, libraries) and public locations (cafés, train stations, airports) are providing wireless environments that facilitate 'anywhere' Internet access. For example, Acadia University (http://www.acadiau.ca/advantage/) has provided all its students with laptops so that they can access information in the classroom areas, social spaces and living accommodation. Other universities, and increasingly schools, are providing the wireless environments but leaving the choice of connection device to the students.

Arguably it is mobile computing, through cell phones, personal digital assistants (PDAs) and portable computers, that is on the verge of achieving the next major leap in accessibility of the Internet. We will return to this in Chapter 7.

Consortium-based e-Learning

The integration of computer-based learning in education currently often takes the form of blended learning where face-to-face courses are offered in classrooms and online e-Learning augments and enriches the students' experience. In a growing number of cases, institutions and training organizations provide entire courses online (see, for example, the University of Phoenix website at http://www.phoenix.edu/online_learning/); indeed, some are exclusively e-Learning based. Taking this a step further is the notion of institutions combining in consortia to provide online courses. At the moment these have yet to prove successful but as each university offers its courses online, a framework for international accreditation will be increasingly attractive and necessary. Factors such as escalating international competition in the provision of education and training and the emergence of franchising models, in which universities engage local partners in overseas locations to administer and deliver their courses, will all serve to push universities to collaborate and build a more flexible exchange of credits. Examples are developing across the higher education sectors of North America and Europe. For example, Carndean University (http://www.unext.com/) hosts a high-powered consortium of business studies-related courses from Stanford, Carnegie-Mellon, London School of Economics, Columbia and Chicago universities.

Throughout this chapter the types of community ventures and contexts have ranged from classroom groups, through groups sharing a particular disadvantage to groups of universities sharing resources to provide e-Learning on a wider basis. The communal base is the key to all these online e-Learning activities and others not mentioned, and the next chapter considers how e-Learning theory accommodates this important feature.

5 e-Learning Theory – Communal Constructivism

The types of changes in education discussed in the previous chapter will undoubtedly command the full attention of theorists from all the education-related disciplines as they attempt to inform policy by explaining and predicting the trends and developments. Learning theory itself is prime for development and this chapter addresses an area on which e-Learning is beginning to impact. Socio-constructivism underpins our understanding of how individuals learn in a social context and extends to the learning organization, which by the nature of its individual members learning together, improves its activities through collective reflection and sharing of experience. e-Learning takes the concept of 'community of learners' a considerable step forward by enabling less formal communities, that is, less formal than the organizational structure of business enterprises or a school or university would imply, to create a self-sustaining communal learning environment. We call this extension to the range of socio-constructivist variants 'communal constructivism' (Holmes et al., 2001), a process in which individuals not only learn socially but contribute their learning to the creation of a communal knowledge base for other learners. Online learning affords them the linked community, the knowledge bases, the knowledge-creation tools and the facility to provide their learning for others. However, before dealing with it specifically it is important to consider the broader theoretical issues.

THE THEORETICAL UNDERPINNING OF ε-LEARNING

e-Learning has the potential to overcome some of the limitations of traditional learning, including, most importantly, the fixed times and locations for learning. It allows for a synergy between advances in information and communication technologies and twenty-first century learning needs or skills, each giving the other a push to explore what is possible and what may ultimately be achieved. However, e-Learning is still considered by many to be simply an add-on to key developments in the technology itself. And it is true to some extent. For example, webcam developments have not been driven by educational needs but educationalists have embraced the technology to use it in learning contexts. On the other hand, the communication and educational needs of the partially sighted have driven the development of ever more effective screen-reader packages. e-Learning may be fundamentally technology-dependent but this does not mean that it has no theoretical underpinning. The concepts comprising e-Learning have emerged from a number of different traditions and fields, notably from education itself and from psychology, computer science and sociology.

There has also been a long tradition of exploring educational technology, where technology is taken to include 'tools' such as curriculum design, learning objectives and pedagogical techniques, and so on. 'Educational technology' studies today are largely confined to curriculum and assessment developments, and tools that enhance learning and teaching. The search is on for new ways of teaching and learning that address the creation of learning environments, and that support students' acquisition of the learning skills needed for the information age. Learning with and not about technology is key. Central to this philosophy is the view that the contribution which information and communication technologies can make to learning is not an end in itself; rather it is their role in motivating and facilitating broader learning experiences that is their key contribution. There is much evidence to support the view that information and communications technologies bring significant added value to education and learning when coupled with such approaches.

From the earliest of human records, teaching and learning has played a key part in the development of our societies. The ancient philosophers in the Eastern and Western traditions, for example Plato, Aristotle and Confucius, were great teachers and have left records of their views on teaching and learning. Key texts such as the Bible and the Koran record the teachings of religious leaders. As in education today, the focus was on individuals, often sitting at the side of their teachers. As the world developed in complexity and population, individual education became the privilege of the elite only, while schools and universities began to emerge to serve larger numbers. However, even these early developments in 'public' education tended to serve only those who could afford to pay for such education. Gradually a societal shift towards a more widely based education provision, and ultimately to free universal education enjoyed in many Western countries today, began to produce a variety of philosophical positions on the meaning and purpose of education and schooling. The culmination of these is the highly diverse 'discipline' of education we know today.

Arguably, knowledge-centred education has been the order of the day for most of the last two millennia. The pursuit of knowledge, in its assimilated forms of facts and understanding, was dominant in most schooling models because the driving influence was the view that all things could be known, classified, sorted and learned to enable humanity to master its environment. These hierarchies of knowledge underpinned the Victorian advances in such natural sciences as physics, astronomy, botany, chemistry and geography – and in applied fields of engineering such as heavy industry, construction and transport. Throughout all this endeavour, the learner and learning experience often took a back seat to the importance attached to what was being taught, and therefore learned. In the last 100 years or so, learning theories have progressively taken centre stage, beginning with Behaviourism, developing through Cognitivism and through to today's widely held Socio-constructivism.

It is not possible to do these great theories justice in a short exposition, but the following outlines should give a flavour of how they have made their contributions to our understanding and implementation of e-Learning today. Before doing so, however, it is crucial to make clear that they are rarely to be considered discrete in an e-Learning context, or indeed in learning more broadly. Arguably all three perspectives occur to some extent in any learning context, with much overlap in activity and in their objective to increase a learner's knowledge. Figure 5.1 illustrates this with one of the most obvious overlapping processes: trial and error.

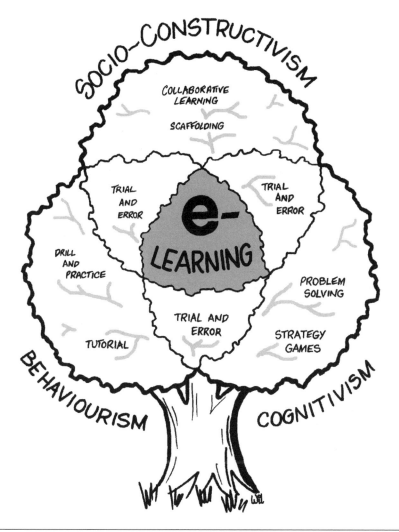

Figure 5.1 Overlapping theoretical underpinnings for e-Learning

Trial and error activities can be simplistic, relying on repetition and success/failure to reinforce learning. They can also be sophisticated exploratory processes in a discovery learning (heuristic) approach, which form parts of individualized problem-solving activities or 'think aloud' collaborative activities. All these trial and error contexts can sit comfortably in aspects of e-Learning designs.

BEHAVIOURISM

Behaviourism is perhaps the oldest and most widely understood of the three main theoretical frameworks underpinning educational and e-Learning theory. The best known proponents of the approach are the twentieth-century psychologists Ivan Pavlov, Burrhus Frederic Skinner, Edward Lee Thorndike and John Broadus Watson. It was Watson who coined the term and he was perhaps the most extreme of the behaviourists in vehemently opposing the notion that a person's mind and consciousness could be used as a focus for explaining behaviour. In essence, classical behaviourism argues that certain stimuli will produce specific reactions in a human or animal; the classic example being Pavlov's dogs, which salivated at the sound of a bell that heralded feeding time. The 'operant' version of behaviourism predicts that with sufficient repetition of an experience, specific behaviours can be 'taught' by reinforcing the desired behaviours with appropriate stimuli.

In this manner, a person will learn a particular behaviour, which they will in future manifest when presented with the appropriate stimulus or experience. The person's capacity for mental processing, through their mind or brain, is effectively irrelevant as the response becomes habituated to the circumstances in which it was cultivated. Much of the early work was carried out with animals, and the behaviour modifications were generally created through exploiting the animals' wish to feed. Elaborate (and sometimes not so elaborate!) experiments were used to 'teach' the animals, most notably the bell-ringing for Pavlov's dogs, which signalled that food was on its way, and the lever-pulling of Thorndike's cats, which brought food within their reach. Skinner 'taught' pigeons to dance with his 'operant' conditioning approach. This ultimately became the dominant learning theory, which based predicted success on the use of rewards as reinforcement stimuli and punishments (or sanctions) as deterrents. Perhaps the most prominent of continuing behaviourist influences in learning today are those associated with the applied behaviour analysis (ABA) approaches to autism-related conditions in children. These use systematic and repetitive techniques to help children to learn purposeful behaviours.

Elsewhere in learning, behaviourist approaches tend to be frowned upon, essentially because they deny a learner-centred dimension to pedagogy by reducing learning to something akin to an automated response. Nevertheless, drill and practice approaches still have their followers in e-Learning contexts, especially for some aspects of mathematics and for the 'quick wins' in revision for examinations such as multiple-choice tests. Tutorials can also be framed as largely behaviourist, especially in systems that purport to 'teach' the content through a tutorial presentation followed by assessment of the learning through focused questions. If the students are unsuccessful, that is, get some of their answers incorrect, the most simplistic systems put them through their tutorial paces again, while more developed systems may give them extension work (for example, more tutorials or external sources of reference). The behaviourist's 'rewards' include progress to the next stage with congratulatory feedback, while the 'sanctions' include repeating the task or doing extension tasks.

COGNITIVISM

The most prominent theorists in the development of cognitivist approaches have been Jean Piaget, Jerome Bruner and Lev Vygotsky. The latter two are also landmark figures in socio-constructivism but their initial work was particularly important in the manner in which it stood in opposition to behaviourist theories. Indeed, it is something of a contrivance on our part to separate cognitivism from socio-constructivism as constructivism itself is a clear link between the two.

Piaget

Cognitivism is something of an antithesis to behaviourism, inasmuch as it focuses squarely on the mind, and the learning processes of the brain. The various strands of the theory are characterized largely by developmental stages, either in the readiness of learners to take on a particular type of learning or in the type of learning itself. For example, Piaget argued that children move through a maturation cycle that governs the type of learning they can accomplish. In the early years the cycle begins with sensory-motor skills (0–2 years: reaching, touching and so on), pre-operational (2–7 years: linguistic development, intuitive understanding of some simple processes) through to concrete operations (7–11 years: organized thinking, problem-solving with 'real' contexts) and formal operations (11–15 years: abstract conceptualization and formal logic). Although heavily criticized, somewhat unfairly, for seeming to promote fixed age ranges for these developmental stages, and for seemingly denying the possibility of any skills being achieved outside the order determined in the linear progression, Piaget's work continues to hold considerable sway in educational theory today.

Bruner

Bruner, too, envisaged a learner's development in terms of a series of steps of increasing learning capability. These steps, in the manner of a staircase, need to be climbed by the learner, implying that some learning capabilities are dependent on the consolidation of others before they can come into play. Other variants of cognitivist theory are also important. For example, David Kolb argues that learning must be experiential. In a development of Kurt Lewin's action research cycle of plan, implement, reflect and then amend the plan, implement new plan and so on, he describes a cycle of four stages of development: a concrete experience, reflection on the experience, abstract conceptualization from the experience and then the trial of the concepts in another situation. The cycle starts anew when the additional experience adds a different dimension to the learning and the learner has cause to reflect, re-conceptualize and test their conceptualization again. David Wood and his colleagues (one of whom was Jerome Bruner) introduced the concept of scaffolding (Wood et al., 1976), another concept based on the climbing or stepwise development of learning.

Scaffolding may be thought of from a learner perspective but is generally considered as part of the tutor's role. From a learner perspective, the learning activities may be framed in a scaffold of progressive steps of achievement. An online tutorial, for example, may be structured in some form of hierarchy or priority, from concrete examples of a learning goal which progressively lead the learner to an abstract understanding of the concepts involved. From the more usual tutor's perspective, scaffolding implies the design of learning experiences, perhaps with appropriate interventions, which are tailored to the learner's readiness to undertake any particular stage of a learning programme. The tutor aims to provide specific tasks that are tailored to the student's current capabilities and which provide stepping stones to the next level of progress. The learner is then able to construct his or her own learning with sufficient resources and activity, progressing smoothly to the desired level of achievement, skill development or understanding.

Vygotsky

Vygotsky is arguably the most influential all of the cognitive theorists, primarily because his work is most linked to the constructivist theories that dominate educational practice today. His theoretical approach is also characterized by developmental stages, in his case two. In contrast to the Piagetian idea that the learner must reach a specific level of development before they can learn in that mode, Vygotsky's thesis relates more to what the learner has the potential to do at any particular time. The theory focuses on the gap between what the learner can do now and what is just beyond their reach; beyond their reach, that is, unless a 'more knowledgeable other' is nearby to assist them to reach the new level of knowledge, skill or understanding. This gap is known as the zone of proximal development (ZPD). Bridging the gap, or 'taking the next step', is very much a learner-centred process in which they have to monitor and regulate their own learning activity. The tutor or perhaps a fellow learner (the more knowledgeable other) is simply a facilitator who may guide them through progressively more challenging learning activities. In e-Learning contexts, the learner may be offered problem-solving or strategic reasoning tasks (both of which often arise in a game format), which place them squarely at the centre of the learning activity with assistance in the ZPD either from software prompts or a (more knowledgeable) tutor or peer.

SOCIO-CONSTRUCTIVISM

The need for assistance from a more knowledgeable other is the conceptual point at which cognitive constructivist theory, in which the learners 'construct' their own knowledge, skills or understanding from their own observational and reasoning capabilities, evolves into the prevailing socio-constructivist theories of today. In essence, the socio-constructivist model requires a third dimension to the interaction between the learners and their environment, that is, other people. These others may be learners or tutors. The developed model includes authentic learning contexts ('contextualized' or 'situated' learning) to foster the learner's motivation through making the learning purposeful and meaningful. The main elements of socio-constructivism may be summarized as learning in a context that is:

- social;
- reflective;
- authentic;
- scaffolded;
- progressive;
- experiential.

The social dimension has led to the rise of concepts such as 'learning organizations', 'learning schools' and 'learning communities', where learning is not only contextualized in the formal settings of schools and universities but also in the wider social community (Holmes, 1999). Such learning contexts are set aside from their 'non-learning' counterpart organizations by the fact that the collective endeavours in reflection, self-evaluation and self-regulation contribute to improvements in the organization's processes and performance. Individuals learn in the company of each other and the organization's corporate goals are addressed by the sharing of their learning through collaboration and co-operation.

This shared learning has been called 'distributed cognition' by Gavriel Salomon and David Perkins, who liken it to a team whose collective performance improves as a result of its members' individual learning, a variant on the whole being greater than the sum of the parts. As Salomon and Perkins (1998) put it:

> Learning to learn in an expanded sense fundamentally involves learning to learn *from* others, learning to learn *with* others, learning to mediate others' learning not only for their own sake but for what that will teach oneself, and learning to contribute to the learning of a collective ... one's contribution to the learning of the collective is likely to benefit the individual as well. (Emphases in original.)

COMMUNAL CONSTRUCTIVISM

'… one's contribution to the learning of the collective is likely to benefit the individual as well'. These words of Salomon and Perkins recognize the learner's contribution to the learning community. But there is a need for an expanded definition of socio-constructivism that takes into account the synergy between the more recent advances in information technology – which are increasing the potential for communication and the ability to store a variety of data types – and some of the educational ideas outlined above. Communal constructivism (Holmes et al., 2001) is the term used throughout this book to denote such an expansion in which e-Learning provides the learners with the tools to create new learning for themselves and to contribute and store their new knowledge, in whatever form it is, projects, artefacts, essays and so on, in a communal knowledge base for the benefit of their community's existing and new learners.

This addition of the learner's newly created knowledge to the communal knowledge base may seem a somewhat contrived extension to socio-constructivism, indeed it might be argued by some that socio-constructivism de facto espouses such a process. However, the original concepts that make up the various strands of the theoretical framework, which is socio-constructivism, were based on a restricted notion of a learner's relatively local learning environment and the social support of a class group. The context of distance learning of earlier years only just breached the one-to-one (student–tutor) environment of basic constructivism, to qualify for socio-constructivism, if the distant learners were afforded opportunities to communicate. However, the ease by which communities of learners today can communicate and learn from each other stretches socio-constructivism much further. e-Learning promotes one-to-one, one-to-many and many-to-many interactions, with hugely magnified opportunities for communal support for learning – and, most importantly, for providing a medium to store and make available the knowledge created by the learners. It is in this specific respect that communal constructivism stretches the socio-constructivism paradigm.

The definition for this communal constructivism, developed from the original version (Holmes et al., 2001), is therefore set out as follows:

Communal constructivism is an approach to learning in which students construct their own knowledge as a result of their experiences and interactions with others, and are afforded the opportunity to contribute this knowledge to a communal knowledge base for the benefit of existing and new learners.

'A river and a pipe'

Two analogies, of water flowing in a river and in a pipe, illustrate the basic tenet of communal constructivism. In the traditional learning model students pass through a learning programme like water flowing through a pipe, with the tutors simply determining a goal, giving its direction and applying the pressure to get there. Once through such a course, there is no trace of them having been on it. Just as a pipe cannot be enriched by water travelling through it, the course remains unaffected by the learning of the students and by the tutors learning from the students. With little or no year-on-year transfer of knowledge between one set of students and the next, there is little prospect of the course itself becoming a dynamic, learning artefact.

In a communal constructivist learning environment, however, the students contribute to the communal knowledge in a permanent form, leaving their own imprint on the course, their school or university, and possibly the discipline – like a river enriching its flood plain each year by adding nutrients and minerals to the soils. The students' learning processes and outputs are captured and harnessed, the course is dynamic and self-generative and builds on new knowledge rather than simply repeating its original content.

The creation of an environment, where students leave their imprint on the course as an integral part of their learning, clearly benefits the learning of their peers in their classes and those that will come after. More importantly, however, it creates a self-sustaining group of existing and future students who appreciate the contribution of their previous peers, and who renew the cycle of communal constructivism by their own engagement and contributions.

Salomon and Perkins distinguish between learning *with* others (the individual learns with and for the team) and learning *from* others (or learning as a result *of* the process). The former addresses the goal of a participative, collective learning while the latter is an individualized, acquisition of learning; the rider being that these cannot be mutually exclusive. An e-Learning community, working in a communally constructivist manner, explicitly sets out to ensure that the two dimensions – individual and collective – are mutually addressed. Each member of the community is 'signed-up' to furthering their own learning in consort with the tutors and other learners and to placing the outcomes of their learning in a communal repository to support other existing and new learners. As their own learning and competence develops, the learners then take on the role of tutors and scaffolders to those less knowledgeable or those who have just joined the community.

An analogy to think of is the doctoral degree, the PhD. Hailing from the top end of the educational spectrum, it is nonetheless a model for the essential aspects of a communal constructivist approach. The concept of PhD study is that of the students making a contribution to the field they are studying. Doctoral students attempt to expand knowledge in a discipline and are encouraged to publish their results so that their own work is recorded and helps develop the field of knowledge. Often they act as post-graduate tutors for undergraduates, passing on their expertise in the field of their study. At doctoral level in the formal education system, the transmission and reception of information is replaced by the process of building new knowledge and making it available to others.

Although many doctoral students, especially in the arts, humanities and social sciences, may find themselves working largely on their own (with a community of fellow learners available perhaps only by electronic means or in occasional conference events), the doctoral study is arguably one of the best learning experiences available, especially if it is undertaken in a team context such as a science research group. Academic fields, renewed and enlivened by publications of new research and scholarly discourse, are self-sustaining and continually growing. So, too, is the archetypal communal constructivist learning environment, which is continually refreshed and sustained by successive learners contributing to the learning resources and the learning activities. Over time the boundaries between learners and tutors begin to blur.

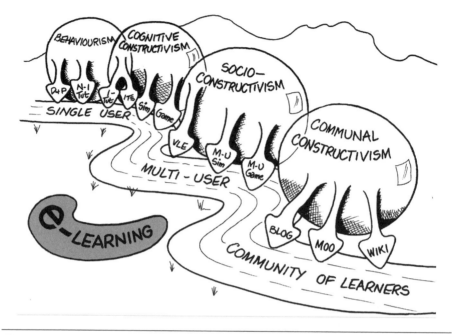

Figure 5.2   Progressive developments in e-Learning from its behaviourist beginnings

TYPES OF e-LEARNING

The various types of e-Learning have followed twin axes of development, characterized by the user context (single user and so on) and the underlying learning theory (behaviourism and so on). Staying with the river analogy, Figure 5.2 illustrates the sequence of development along these axes. The river represents the growing complexity of user engagement from single user to multi-user to community of learners. The distinctly organic 'space hoppers' on the bank of the river represent the major developments in learning theory as the river of user engagement becomes more complex.

As Figure 5.2 illustrates, drill and practice (D&P) and simple non-interactive tutorials (N-I Tut) form the links between single-user modes and the behaviourism hopper. There is an overlap between behaviourism and cognitive constructivism and, in the overlapping zone, interactive tutorials (I-Tut), which allow the learner to 'have a go' at questions and so on, and intelligent tutoring systems (ITS), which allow the learner to work within an expert system model, provide a link to the single-user stretch of the river. Simulations (Sim) and games (Game) make up the main body of this hopper though still on the edge of the single-user section of the flow. The next overlap is between cognitive and socio-constructivism. In this case virtual learning environments, which can facilitate social learning, make the link between both and the first stretch of multi-user flow. More squarely linked to the socio-constructivist hopper, however, are the multi-user variants of simulations (MuSim) and games (MuGame). The next jump is to communal constructivism with the very different forms of e-Learning exemplified by weblogs (blog), multi-user object oriented systems (MOO) and multi-editor wiki systems (wiki). These systems are discussed in more detail later (see Chapter 9 for blogs and wikis) but suffice to say here that, as the figure illustrates, they represent a significant move forward for e-Learning, based on communities of users/learners in a communal constructivist context.

SEEDS OF CHANGE

A diverse range of techniques is needed to enrich a communal constructivist learning environment, to ensure it honours its *raison d'être*: to learn with and for others. Peer tutoring and project-based learning in a group are obvious techniques but many others such as cognitive apprenticeship are also advocated. However, it is clear that some of the fundamental features of the conventional educational process, such as the publishing of information for learners, the physical arrangements for learner engagement (timetables, room allocations and so on) and the assessment of students' learning, will become increasingly vulnerable to change in the face of communal constructivist approaches stimulated by e-learning environments.

e-Learning Design – Concepts and Considerations

Focusing on approaches that support the development of student thought, this chapter sets out design principles for e-Learning that scaffold students' learning by integrating critical thinking and providing 'cognitive apprenticeships'. The central theme, as throughout the book, is the creation of a learning environment informed by communal constructivist theory. Students create their own knowledge from their experiences and from interaction with their environment and other people. They then contribute this new knowledge in the communal knowledge base for the benefit of others. e-Learning must therefore enable learners to construct their own knowledge and understanding in a computer-based environment that allows continual reconstruction and reshaping as their learning develops and they encounter new evidence.

ROLE OF THE TUTOR AS e-LEARNING DESIGNER

The role of any tutor proposing to enable their students to engage in such e-Learning activities begins with the planning phase and continues through the activity itself and on through to a post-delivery review and quality check. In their organizational role the e-tutor acts as a content facilitator, a resource provider and an overall e-Learning activity manager and administrator. It is important, however, also to ensure that in structuring their course, e-tutors create a supportive environment for the diversity of learners they will encounter.

The planning process has a number of key considerations including:

- audience;
- resource needs;
- proposed learning outcomes;
- assessment needs and methods.

Audience

Clearly, tutors must know their audience. They need to have carried out an analysis of the target group's learning needs covering questions such as: what prior learning, relevant to the learning proposed, is in place? Are any special competences needed? If yes, how will these be developed? Throughout the process a constant eye must be kept on the needs and characteristics of the audience to ensure that as good a fit as possible is achieved.

Resource needs

Before undertaking the development of e-Learning material, the tutor will have to know what resources are available and how the students may access them. Online resources will generally be easily accessible but access privileges may need to be arranged. Conventional paper or other media resources, such as textbooks, videos and so on, should be avoided as they will prove more difficult for e-learners to access if they cannot be dispatched on request.

Proposed learning outcomes

Whether conventional or online, any learning and teaching plan must consider the learning outcomes that are being sought. They will often be specific in nature, requiring students to master a particular mathematical concept for example. Or perhaps they will target in more general terms a high-level skill, such as demonstrating an empathetic understanding of the circumstances surrounding the Boston tea party (see Box 6.1)! Still other outcomes will be largely expressive, requiring students to engage in a particular learning task that might involve a creative activity such as painting or writing a poem. Whatever the learning outcome, and whatever its specificity or generality or indeed its complexity, tutors must be clear about the learning in which they wish their students to engage.

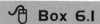 **Box 6.1**

Eyewitness accounts are often used in history studies to engage the learner more authentically with the historical context. The website http://www.historyplace.com/unitedstates/revolution/teaparty.htm, for example, provides an eyewitness account of the events surrounding the Boston tea party. To develop a sense of how this type of activity might engage the history student, take a look at the statement of George Hewes, who dressed himself as a Native American, complete with war paint and tomahawk, to attack the tea-ships commando-style!

Assessment needs and methods

If the e-Learning course has to be assessed, for example, for a reporting or accreditation purpose, the tutor should consider how best the assessment can be made online. Perhaps the students have to take tests, create portfolios or submit assignments. All these are routine in an e-Learning environment. Remember, though, that most of the 'subjectively' assessed work, such as essays, assignments, project reports, and so on, all require the 'human' touch. The e-Learning system has a relatively limited 'messenger' role in the former, enabling interaction between the tutor and the students for issuing grades and providing feedback. There are well-developed means of having the computer do the first-line marking of more 'objective' modes of testing, such as multiple-choice or structured questions. Note also, that learning outcomes involving physical artefacts (such as artwork) or performance (such as dramatic cameos) will clearly oblige the tutor to resort to conventional physical submission or the attendance of the student in person. However, for the large majority of contexts there should be relatively few circumstances in which the e-Learning environment cannot facilitate the submission or assessment of student work. There is no substitute for thorough planning of how the system should address assessment needs.

INSTRUCTIONAL DESIGN

The key to the success of the personal computer in education is the freedom it gives learners to create and manage their own learning. Information and communications technologies allow people to develop their thoughts and share them with others in a variety of ways including chat rooms, bulletin boards and weblogs. However, for tutors in schools, colleges and universities the majority of e-Learning opportunities and resources are probably ready-made, that is, designed and populated with content by someone else. Next best are the systems that are ready-made in a structural sense, for example, the templates provided by virtual learning environment vehicles such as Blackboard, Moodle and WebCT, which allow the tutors to populate them with content appropriate to their student groups. Increasingly, however, tutors are taking on the role of 'instructional designers' or e-tutors, spurred on by the increasingly user-friendly and sophisticated design tools offered by these types of systems. Turning good pedagogical ideas into solid online e-Learning is the challenge that faces them. The level of interest has rejuvenated the established field of educational technology (a field concerned as much about pedagogy and design of curricula as it is about the tools available to tutors) and a new quasi-discipline is forming around 'instructional design'. In essence, Instructional Design is a branch of knowledge concerned with research and theory about learning and teaching strategies, and the processes for developing and implementing these strategies, particularly in an e-Learning environment.

The creation of quality e-Learning and teaching materials involves the development, implementation, evaluation and maintenance of environments that facilitate the target learning. According to Murphy (1997), the best of such environments are constructivist in design and ethos, where

- Goals and objectives are derived by the student or in negotiation with the teacher, or system;
- Teachers serve in the role of guides, monitors, coaches, tutors and facilitators;
- Knowledge construction and not reproduction is emphasized;
- This construction takes place in individual contexts and through social negotiation, collaboration and experience;
- Collaborative and cooperative learning are favoured in order to expose the learner to alternative viewpoints;
- Scaffolding is facilitated to help students perform just beyond the limits of their ability;
- Assessment is authentic and interwoven with teaching.

The Constructivist learning processes often accommodated by contextualized or situated learning approaches, which engage multiple perspectives (student, tutor, external 'expert' and so on), authentic activities (analysis of primary data or interpretation from primary sources) and real-world environments (for example, problem-solving in the workplace) as means of challenging learners to develop their own knowledge and understanding. One conceptualization of this complex learning environment is that of 'cognitive apprenticeship'.

COGNITIVE APPRENTICESHIPS

The concept of a cognitive apprenticeship was first articulated by Allan Collins, John Seely Brown and Susan Newman in 1989 (Collins et al., 1989) and it remains very apt for e-Learning today. As the name suggests, it uses many of the instructional strategies of traditional apprenticeships but emphasizes cognitive rather than physical skills. In essence, Collins, Brown and Holum (1991) argue that in an apprenticeship context the processes or outcomes of thinking, for example the physical activities of the craftsperson or garment-maker, are made visible. The challenge for the conventional learning context is to make the thinking visible, and cognitive apprenticeships are based on this central pursuit.

Collins et al. (1991) argued that the traditional model of apprenticeship comprises four processes: modelling, scaffolding, fading and coaching.

Modelling

The apprentice observes as the expert craftsperson models, that is, demonstrates, a practical activity such as fashioning a wood joint. The expert carries out the task in a sequence that is geared to fit the apprentice's level of ability, while explaining what is being done and why it is being done that way. Having observed the expert, the apprentice then attempts a similar task, with the expert providing hints and corrective feedback.

Scaffolding

Scaffolding is the term coined by Wood et al. (1976) to describe a process in which learners are assisted to reach new levels of knowledge, skill or understanding, which are currently just beyond their reach. The analogy is of a support structure, a scaffold, which enables a person to stretch and climb to places that would otherwise be beyond their reach. The expert reaches out to the apprentices and assists them when they need just a little bit of help to take the next step in their learning. In learning theory this is often referred to as the 'zone of proximal development' first conceptualized in the 1920s by Lev Vygotsky (in translation, 1978). In the zone of proximal development, learners have an established base of knowledge, skills and understanding but may need an expert or 'more knowledgeable other' to provide measured assistance and guidance to help them improve. The role of the expert is therefore one of observing where and when a helping hand is needed, and of deciding the extent of the help required. Appropriate and timely support can allow students to function at the changing edge of their individual development.

Fading

As the apprentice becomes more skilled in a task, the expert begins to transfer responsibility to them by 'fading' into the background. The disengagement is slow and never complete, that is, the apprentices continue to progress at their own pace but remain able to call upon the expert if needed. For their part, experts progressively take more of a 'watching brief', judging when an intervention might be helpful without undermining the apprentice's confidence.

Coaching

Coaching pervades all the processes, with the expert continually prompting the apprentice by 'choosing tasks, providing hints and scaffolding, evaluating the activities … and diagnosing the kinds of problems they are having, challenging them and offering encouragement, giving feedback, structuring the ways to do things, working on particular weaknesses' (Collins et al., 1991: 9).

Collins et al. (1991) argue that the interplay between observation, scaffolding and fading helps to develop more generic benefits in 'self monitoring and correction skills and in integrating the skills and conceptual knowledge needed to advance towards expertise' (1991: 9). While some aspects of the traditional model of apprenticeship might be said to be behaviourist – take, for example, the 'practice makes perfect' ethos of drill and practice – the features of a constructivist approach are clearly evident in such aspects as the learner trying things out; thereby learning both from successes and mistakes.

Conventional learning contexts, for example the university or school classroom, can utilize the constructivist features of observation by students, their learning by doing and the scaffolding by tutors (experts). Tutors can also find ways to 'remove' the scaffolding sufficiently for the learners to consolidate their learning and move on, leaving the tutors to 'fade' away on the particular aspect of learning that the learners have now achieved. The cycle then begins again in another task context, as the learners strive to reach yet a higher level of achievement. Ultimately, the tutor must aim to set increasingly complex tasks to ensure an upwards trajectory in learning, a trajectory that fosters higher-order skills such as problem-solving, critical thinking, reflection, analysis and synthesis.

But some additional and very important features of the traditional apprenticeship model can also prove to be of significant benefit. Apprenticeship is often characterized by its 'on the job' context, that is, learning that is made authentic by being 'contextualized' or 'situated' in the apprentice's working environment. This learning also takes place in a social context with other people who may be either experts or apprentices themselves. The benefits of a situated learning environment of this kind include the opportunity for apprentices to observe and be guided by more than one expert and by peers who in any one skill may be 'more knowledgeable others'. They also engage in 'real' tasks associated with the job for which they are training. In arguing for a learning approach based on a 'cognitive' apprenticeship, Collins et al. (1991), argued there are three main differences with the traditional model:

- The thinking of the learners and teachers must be made 'visible', just as the processes and outcomes of thinking by experts and vocational apprentices are physically observable in traditional apprenticeships.
- The abstract tasks of the learning content in conventional curricula must be made meaningful to the learners, that is, they must be situated or contextualized in ways to which students can relate.
- The learning process must address transferability. While traditional apprentices may develop task-specific skills (in carpentry or other practical trades, for example) cognitive apprentices must be enabled to develop generic skills, which transfer across contexts and tasks.

These can be tough challenges for the tutor but the power of the computer renders some of them much more possible in the realms of e-Learning environments than in the traditional classroom.

DESIGN ISSUES FOR ε-LEARNING

Any successful learning environment will be characterized by a number of features relating to how learners engage with their learning and how this is supported by the tutor. An e-Learning environment is essentially no different except in the important triangularity of the learner–computer–tutor interaction, where the 'computer' part in the phrase is a simple way of denoting the technical complexity of an e-Learning environment. The features relating to the learner, tutor and e-Learning environment, which have significant importance for designers of e-Learning, include:

- developing higher-order skills;
- developing the capacity for self-assessment and reflection;
- fostering motivation;

- encouraging curiosity;
- promoting understanding of learning goals and assessment criteria;
- recognizing achievement;
- scaffolding 'next steps';
- supporting different learning styles;
- incorporating learner activity;
- creating an authentic learning environment;
- creating a social learning environment;
- creating links in learning activities.

These are outlined briefly below before turning to the types of e-Learning activities that encapsulate them to varying degrees.

Developing higher-order skills

Separate from the relatively easily assimilated skills of description, collation and transmission of information are what are termed higher-order skills. These are crucially important in any learning context and include:

- learners searching for information using criteria that have been identified as relevant to the task;
- analysing information and synthesizing new meanings from it;
- solving problems by combinations of heuristics (discovery, trial and error) and analysis;
- applying ideas and information creatively to develop new knowledge;
- generalizing from specific cases;
- hypothesizing and testing;
- planning and strategizing;
- evaluating and critiquing ideas and knowledge;
- reaching reasoned conclusions.

Clearly this is a formidable 'shopping list' for any learning environment to address but e-Learning design should always aim to encapsulate good practice and in this context the list items are not unreasonable.

Developing the capacity for self-assessment and reflection

A cross-cutting theme in all learning is the aim for all learners to become autonomous lifelong learners. There will always be situations in which learners find they are 'on their own', in a learning context that has no inbuilt or convenient social support or which is not facilitated by an e-Learning network. Being an autonomous learner, that is, being able to seek out the necessary information and knowledge without help, is a crucial factor in sustaining continued learning. In a similar fashion, without external judges of the quality or extent of the learning, skills of self-assessment and reflection are crucial in order for learners to be able to guide themselves in determining 'where they are' in their learning and what the next steps should be. e-Learning systems, which promote self-assessment and reflection, should ensure that they have key elements of the interaction geared towards guiding the learners to undertake evaluation of their own progress and planning their next steps.

Fostering motivation

Learners will manifest different levels and types of motivation, ranging from the 'intrinsic' to the 'extrinsic'. Intrinsic motivation derives from internalized factors such as the pleasure of learning itself or the sense of achievement. Extrinsic motivation will generally comprise external factors such as the approval of tutors and the esteem in which the learners feel they are held by their peers. It may also simply involve a reward such as a qualification or a penalty, such as non-progress to the next stage of a course. Regardless of the nature of the primary motivation under which a learner operates, it is widely accepted that interesting, attractive and challenging (within 'reach') environments will motivate their engagement. Constructive, meaningful feedback is another major feature of a motivational environment. In an e-Learning environment, relatively superficial attractiveness and interest can be created through judicious use of space, colour, animation and sound. More sophisticated systems will have well-developed interactional features offering meaningful feedback in terms of what is going wrong or right, and links to tutors or other learners who can offer more direct feedback.

Encouraging curiosity

> Make your child attentive to the phenomena of nature; soon you will make him curious. But to nurture his curiosity, never hasten to satisfy it. Put questions within his reach and let him solve them himself. Let him know nothing because you have told him, but because he has learnt it for himself. Let him not be taught science, let him invent it. (Rousseau, 1762: para. 564)

Rousseau's exhortation is to encourage curiosity and discovery learning (and with the 'put questions within his reach' there are also allusions to the much later concept of the zone of proximal development). It is a reasonably secure observation that when people are curious about something, that is, they want to know about it, they will spend time and energy applying themselves to the quest. And when they have no interest in the something, learning about it is far from their first priority. Ask secondary school mathematics teachers about the level of curiosity they can engender about solving quadratic equations!

Generating curiosity on the part of a learner can be a key ingredient in fostering learning, though not required in every instance of course, and e-Learning approaches can harness it quite effectively. A good example is the UK National History Museum site, Mission Explore at http://www.nhm.ac.uk/kids-only/fun-games/mission-explore/. Students request a special permit to explore a country called Regaloam and they 'travel' to it to collect specimens for the museum. Once they are in Regaloam, they can choose to explore a variety of natural history aspects including fossils and insect life. They choose where in the region to search and ultimately find something, as yet un-named but with a picture. They return to the museum to search out details of their specimen.

Promoting understanding of learning goals and assessment criteria

There is nothing worse that being engaged on a course that is confusing and difficult to follow because no one has taken the time to establish and

ng addressed and how these
chools, colleges and universi-
pite the rise of constructivist
ings promote a negotiation
ery and assessment methods.
orgivable oversight because,
tutor will probably be asked
ultimately 'switch off' if they
rning activities are directed.
utset to provide details of the
or example, analysing themes
ens, to the general, for exam-
ticism. They will also indicate
sometimes with illustrative
y with the detailed rubrics of

a 'pat on the back' for carry-
om, some students do very
ir work while others may do
of approval from their peers
can excel, indeed that some
otivational issue that implies
ve for those who do not have
e a bigger impact. Success,
onsolidated to ensure that it
decline in motivation and
t. Ensuring recognition of all
to be relatively easy in a
e-based feedback commen-
lications of insensitive body
or. Designing machine-based
while online tutor or peer

Scaffolding 'next steps'

A central tenet of constructivist appro
learning that a 'more knowledgeable
peer) can provide when a learner is n
knowledge, skill or understanding. Th
when the tutor guides the learner t
become progressively more complex a
goal, or it can be ad hoc when the wa
intervention will assist the learner to r
progress. As we outlined earlier, this
folding', the construction of a frame of
and partially by the learner, in which th
is accomplished by their own 'climbing
or peer. At each point in the frame, th
themselves know what the next step
process a tutor specifically must kno
assist appropriately. In some fixed con
is the danger that these steps and
restricted, hindering some learners wh
munal constructivist environments, wit
tively, judgements on next steps and wh
focused.

Supporting different learning

Given that e-Learning specifically facili
ences, Howard Gardner's advice on
relevant in tailoring delivery and experi
ferences. Gardner first put forward the
different types or 'multiple' intelligen
healthy debate over the idea since. He
intelligences, later increased to nine
various abilities of any individual – each
levels in each individual. The nine int

Developing the capacity for self-assessment and reflection

A cross-cutting theme in all learning is the aim for all learners to become autonomous lifelong learners. There will always be situations in which learners find they are 'on their own', in a learning context that has no inbuilt or convenient social support or which is not facilitated by an e-Learning network. Being an autonomous learner, that is, being able to seek out the necessary information and knowledge without help, is a crucial factor in sustaining continued learning. In a similar fashion, without external judges of the quality or extent of the learning, skills of self-assessment and reflection are crucial in order for learners to be able to guide themselves in determining 'where they are' in their learning and what the next steps should be. e-Learning systems, which promote self-assessment and reflection, should ensure that they have key elements of the interaction geared towards guiding the learners to undertake evaluation of their own progress and planning their next steps.

Fostering motivation

Learners will manifest different levels and types of motivation, ranging from the 'intrinsic' to the 'extrinsic'. Intrinsic motivation derives from internalized factors such as the pleasure of learning itself or the sense of achievement. Extrinsic motivation will generally comprise external factors such as the approval of tutors and the esteem in which the learners feel they are held by their peers. It may also simply involve a reward such as a qualification or a penalty, such as non-progress to the next stage of a course. Regardless of the nature of the primary motivation under which a learner operates, it is widely accepted that interesting, attractive and challenging (within 'reach') environments will motivate their engagement. Constructive, meaningful feedback is another major feature of a motivational environment. In an e-Learning environment, relatively superficial attractiveness and interest can be created through judicious use of space, colour, animation and sound. More sophisticated systems will have well-developed interactional features offering meaningful feedback in terms of what is going wrong or right, and links to tutors or other learners who can offer more direct feedback.

Encouraging curiosity

> Make your child attentive to the phenomena of nature; soon you will make him curious. But to nurture his curiosity, never hasten to satisfy it. Put questions within his reach and let him solve them himself. Let him know nothing because you have told him, but because he has learnt it for himself. Let him not be taught science, let him invent it. (Rousseau, 1762: para. 564)

Rousseau's exhortation is to encourage curiosity and discovery learning (and with the 'put questions within his reach' there are also allusions to the much later concept of the zone of proximal development). It is a reasonably secure observation that when people are curious about something, that is, they want to know about it, they will spend time and energy applying themselves to the quest. And when they have no interest in the something, learning about it is far from their first priority. Ask secondary school mathematics teachers about the level of curiosity they can engender about solving quadratic equations!

Generating curiosity on the part of a learner can be a key ingredient in fostering learning, though not required in every instance of course, and e-Learning approaches can harness it quite effectively. A good example is the UK National History Museum site, Mission Explore at http://www.nhm.ac.uk/kids-only/fun-games/mission-explore/. Students request a special permit to explore a country called Regaloam and they 'travel' to it to collect specimens for the museum. Once they are in Regaloam, they can choose to explore a variety of natural history aspects including fossils and insect life. They choose where in the region to search and ultimately find something, as yet un-named but with a picture. They return to the museum to search out details of their specimen.

Promoting understanding of learning goals and assessment criteria

There is nothing worse that being engaged on a course that is confusing and difficult to follow because no one has taken the time to establish and communicate what learning outcomes are being addressed and how these may be assessed. In conventional classrooms (schools, colleges and universities) this type of situation is not unheard of, despite the rise of constructivist learning approaches, which among other things promote a negotiation between learners and tutors on curriculum delivery and assessment methods. However, in e-Learning contexts it is an unforgivable oversight because, unlike the conventional classroom where the tutor will probably be asked about such issues by the students, learners will ultimately 'switch off' if they cannot quickly determine to what end the learning activities are directed. Most e-Learning systems will take time at the outset to provide details of the learning goals they address, from the specific, for example, analysing themes of social despair in the writings of Charles Dickens, to the general, for example, learning how to use the tools of literary criticism. They will also indicate how the work of the course will be assessed, sometimes with illustrative examples of tasks and assignments but generally with the detailed rubrics of the assessment methods being used.

Recognizing achievement

There are few learners who do not appreciate a 'pat on the back' for carrying out a task well. In the conventional classroom, some students do very well and receive considerable plaudits for their work while others may do more modestly, with a consequent lower level of approval from their peers and teachers. Recognizing that not everyone can excel, indeed that some will make very little progress at all, is a key motivational issue that implies that feedback must be sensitive and constructive for those who do not have the skills or intellectual wherewithal to make a bigger impact. Success, however low level, must be recognized and consolidated to ensure that it can grow and not fall into the often rapid decline in motivation and achievement that a spiral of failure can prompt. Ensuring recognition of all levels of achievement is often considered to be relatively easy in a computer-based environment because machine-based feedback commentaries are de facto untrammelled by the complications of insensitive body language or choice of words of the human tutor. Designing machine-based feedback must reflect a positive demeanour, while online tutor or peer feedback may need to be moderated.

Scaffolding 'next steps'

A central tenet of constructivist approaches is the powerful assistance to learning that a 'more knowledgeable other' (a tutor or more advanced peer) can provide when a learner is near to achieving a particular level of knowledge, skill or understanding. The situation can be stage-managed when the tutor guides the learner through a framework of tasks that become progressively more complex and directed to the ultimate learning goal, or it can be ad hoc when the watchful tutor decides that a judicious intervention will assist the learner to reach the next step in their learning progress. As we outlined earlier, this process is often described as 'scaffolding', the construction of a frame of knowledge development by a tutor, and partially by the learner, in which the learner's progress to higher levels is accomplished by their own 'climbing' or with the helping hand of a tutor or peer. At each point in the frame, the more knowledgeable other must themselves know what the next step is, and in planning the scaffolding process a tutor specifically must know the likely next steps, in order to assist appropriately. In some fixed content e-Learning environments there is the danger that these steps and the scaffolded frame may be very restricted, hindering some learners while accelerating others, but in communal constructivist environments, with tutors and peers working interactively, judgements on next steps and when to intervene will likely be better focused.

Supporting different learning styles

Given that e-Learning specifically facilitates individualized learning experiences, Howard Gardner's advice on multiple intelligences is particularly relevant in tailoring delivery and experience to accommodate individual differences. Gardner first put forward the idea that learners possess a range of different types or 'multiple' intelligences in 1983 and there has been a healthy debate over the idea since. He proposed a combination of seven intelligences, later increased to nine (Kearsley, 2003), that embody the various abilities of any individual – each ability manifesting itself at different levels in each individual. The nine intelligences comprise those that are perhaps more commonly recognized, such as spatial, linguistic, musical and logical-mathematical, and more novel intelligences such as bodily kinaesthetic, naturalist, interpersonal, intrapersonal and existential.

🐭 Box 6.2

Howard Gardner's books on multiple intelligences are widely available, but for a quick overview go to the US-based Public Broadcasting Service website http://www.pbs.org/wnet/gperf/education/ed_mi_overview.html. The site provides examples that help to explain what each of the intelligences means.

Critics have argued that multiple intelligence theory merely reworks an age-old recognition of talents. However, whether talents, intelligences or skills, if individuals do have greater or lesser levels of discrete types of these entities, then Gardner's theory suggests that any learning materials design should be as flexible as possible to meet the diverse needs of all learners. e-Learning environments are capable of considerable customization and just as conventional learning materials and approaches must be amenable to a diversity of learners, e-Learning design should also address the flexibility needed for a wide range of learning styles and needs.

Kolb's learning style inventory (LSI), as mentioned earlier, is also a helpful means of planning e-Learning. Put simply, it proposes that learning takes place by receiving and processing information. He identified four different ways a student may learn – as an accommodator, diverger, assimilator and/or converger (Kolb, 1994). Students and tutors can investigate their own learning styles by examining how they 'fit' a learning styles inventory, normally created by presenting dichotomous types of style. For example, a person may learn better in a 'visual' context than from 'verbal' tuition. One example of an inventory, from Felder and Soloman (2005), is presented in abbreviated form in Table 6.1 (see http://www.ncsu.edu/felder-public/ILSdir/styles.htm for fuller details of the learning style inventory) but note that most people will have styles comprising levels of each pole of the learning preferences.

Table 6.1 Summary of Felder and Soloman's 'Learning styles and strategies' (2005)

Learning style dimension	Description of learning preference poles	
Active/Reflective	ACTIVE learners tend to retain and understand information best by doing something active with it – discussing or applying it or explaining it to others	REFLECTIVE learners prefer to think about it quietly first
Sensing/Intuitive	SENSING learners tend to like learning facts	INTUITIVE learners often prefer discovering possibilities and relationships
Visual/Verbal	VISUAL learners remember best what they see – pictures, diagrams, flow charts, time lines, films and demonstrations	VERBAL learners get more out of words – written and spoken explanations. Everyone learns more when information is presented both visually and verbally
Sequential/Global	SEQUENTIAL learners tend to gain understanding in linear steps, with each step following logically from the previous one	GLOBAL learners tend to learn in large jumps, absorbing material almost randomly without seeing connections, and then suddenly understanding it

---

Box 6.3

Find out about your own learning style by going to Barbara Soloman's and Richard Felder's Index of Learning Styles questionnaire at http://www.engr.ncsu.edu/learningstyles/ilsweb.html.

There are a number of resources on the Internet that link to learning styles. Try out some online diagnostic tools and learning styles

(Continued)

tests on the Learning Disability Pride site at http://www.ldpride.net/
learningstyles.MI.htm, a site conceived by Liz Bogod, a person with
learning disability. The basic premise of the site is that if you know
your learning style you can develop strategies to assist you in building
up your weaker areas and promoting your strengths.

Incorporating learner activity

Unlike a didactic classroom environment, such as the transmission mode of
teaching which is so typical of many university lectures for example,
e-Learning almost without exception guarantees learners' practical engagement even if it is as basic as drill and practice or tutorial. However, more
sophisticated e-Learning environments (and to be fair, more innovative
lecturing styles) will enable a broader learner engagement through a
demand for creative responses or the completion of tasks requiring the
searching for and analysing of information. Decision-making, problem-
solving and hypothesis-testing are all aspects of active learning in which the
learner may be asked to engage. Interaction with peers and tutors in a
social learning context online will also ensure a degree of higher-order
skills activity, including the sharing of ideas and formulation of questions.

Creating an authentic learning environment

The relatively abstract contexts for much classroom learning activity are less
conducive to students' learning than the learning opportunities offered by
the workplace or by contexts that deliberately make the learning meaningful or purposeful. In the traditional classroom, meaningfulness and 'reality'
are often contrived, with notable success, through simulations and role
plays, for example. However, e-Learning environments can arguably do
much better. With the benefits of multimedia, animation and advanced
communication facilities, e-Learning can place the learner in a simulated
'virtual' environment approximating to the 'real' thing, or can engage them
through webcam, Internet telephony and whiteboard technologies, for

example, with distant laboratories, field trips or events and so on. Such contexts can indeed be much more than 'authentic'; they can actually be 'real', in the sense of the learner engaging with actual events and processes (see, for example, the Jason project at http://www.jasonproject.org/ or the PEARL project below).

Creating a social learning environment

Just as scaffolding is a tenet of constructivism, a social environment for learning, in which the learner has the support of tutors and other learners like themselves, is the defining element of social constructivism. Online e-Learning environments almost always have an element of social interaction to support learning, through asynchronous email communications at the least, but increasingly more often through synchronous text, audio and video communication. The more support a learner feels they have, whether through access to several tutors, external experts or peer colleagues on the same course, the more likely they will be well disposed to the course and will succeed.

Creating links in learning activities

Traditional teaching will often set a goal of generalizing specific learning to wider contexts. This is often achieved through broadening the resource base on which the students can apply their skills and understandings, and through extending the variety of learning-related tasks and assignments themselves. e-Learning must do this also and is perhaps increasingly more able to do so with the huge resources available on the Internet. Indeed, it is probably the case that extension activities in the traditional classroom are now more and more directed to Internet sources than textbooks or other static sources available to the tutor.

TYPES OF LEARNING ENGAGEMENT

Several types of learning engagement can encompass some or all aspects of this extensive array of pedagogical considerations for designing an e-Learning environment, and these include case studies, problem-based learning, gaming, simulation and WebQuests. These are outlined below.

Virtual case studies, fieldwork and experimental laboratories

Case studies in business education have been around since the 1920s, when they were first introduced by the Harvard Business School. They remain one of the most important pedagogical approaches in business education today. The programmes focus on the virtual boardroom, creating a business decision-making environment in much the same manner as an actual case study in a university classroom, that is, students at a distance have to research their role, the business context and the decisions that need to be made. Using an e-Learning context the decisions can be part of discussions with other students and tutors, and their implications can be tested online. Such case studies stress active participation in learning. i-CASE, for example, provides a suite of interactive and multimedia case studies for university business schools covering real cases such as 'British Petroleum in South Wales' and 'Union Carbide – Kanawha Valley' (see http://www.i-case.com/newweb/index.htm).

Virtual fieldwork environments and experimental laboratories also cover many of the key pedagogical aspirations and come in two main variants: those in which the students control a real situation remotely and those which simulate an experimental context and which allow students to learn from the manipulation of real data. An example of the former is the PEARL project (Colwell et al., 2002), which provided access to experiments in university laboratories that students with disabilities could not otherwise attend. The experiments at four universities (Open University, Trinity College, Dublin, University of Porto, Portugal and University of Dundee) involved remote flame testing, printed circuit board testing, cell behaviour and digital circuit design. An example of the latter is the University of Florida's virtual field laboratory for environmental studies at http://3dmodel.ifas.ufl.edu. This site allows students to explore different environmental aspects of the university's own 42-hectare 'flatwood', albeit with some 'limitations', namely, the lack of 'landscape experiences such as mosquitoes, humidity and getting dirty' (Ramasundaram et al., 2005).

Online problem-based learning

Problem-based learning (PBL) can be used in an online environment as a teaching strategy to enable learners to acquire thinking and inquiry skills as well as information. It is characterized by the presentation of a problem, puzzle or dilemma, followed by the students being asked to explore solutions with varying degrees of support from their tutors. A well-developed example of the genre is the Classrooms of the Future project and site (http://www.cotf. edu/), hosted by the Wheeling Jesuit University and funded by the US National Aeronautics and Space Administration. With access to the rich data resources of NASA, the site enables students to identify a problem, such as preserving biodiversity in the rainforests. For each context, the site uses a problem-solving template (at http://www.cotf.edu/ete/ pbl.html), which asks the students to:

- read and analyse the problem scenario;
- list what is known;
- develop a problem statement;
- list what is needed;
- list possible actions;
- analyse information;
- present findings.

The scope for some of the template actions to be iterative, repetitive or concurrent is emphasized, as is the need to reflect back on the original articulation of the problem statement as new knowledge and understanding is created.

Box 6.4

Explore the problems presented in attempts to track and predict the trajectories of hurricanes in the USA by visiting http://www.cotf.edu/ete/ modules/sevweath/swhurricanewatch.html. Also visit the team training resources at http://www.cotf.edu/ete/modules/sevweath/swtracking-preview.html, which include satellite-tracking videos from NASA's archives, and then follow the problem-based learning template as you take up the 'contract' to track a hurricane.

Online simulations and gaming

Simulations and games are well renowned for assisting learners to connect theory and practice through innovative and usually (but not always!) interesting approaches. Simulations are models of real-life practice and help break down problems into discrete and manageable parts. e-Learning environments, which capitalize on a simulation approach, can allow the learner to interact with a system that is based on the steps needed to be taken to solve a type of given problem. Gaming environments are often similar to simulations but tend to involve a level of competition and are generally used to increase motivation for simulations. An example of a source that marries the two aspects of simulations and gaming is Lavamind at http://www.lavamind.com. Lavamind provide a downloadable, free shareware version of their main title, Gazillionaire. This intergalactic trading company game simulates the main features of market conditions and is designed to motivate students with its zany graphics and player roles. SimCity, at simcity.ea.com is one of the longest established strategy and planning games. Students build a virtual city by developing it from 'scratch' with utilities, news media, emergency services, leisure facilities, hospitals, police, residential and commercial areas, and of course the Sims (the inhabitants) themselves. Dealing with boom and bust, natural disasters and social crises are all part of the decision-making environment in which students have to develop strategies and manage the municipal budget and taxation. The online site encourages participation in chat events and talking to fellow members of the SimCity community.

WebQuests

In the words of the Wikipedia definition:

> The WebQuest is valued as a highly constructivist teaching method, meaning that students are 'turned loose' to find, synthesize, and analyze information in a hands-on fashion, actively constructing their own understanding of the material. WebQuests' focus on group work also makes them popular examples of cooperative learning. (http://en.wikipedia.org/wiki/Webquest)

The idea was launched by Bernie Dodge of the University of California at San Diego in 1995 and has grown into a widely used means of engaging students in many of the higher-order skills listed above. The simple template structure is much favoured by schoolteachers especially and requires the learning environment to be structured in six sections: the Introduction (introducing the context), the Task (the students must complete), the Process (the students must use to complete the task, including the roles they must investigate and take on), the Evaluation (of the students' learning, in terms of rubric, grading scales and so on – usually termed 'assessment' in the UK), the Conclusion (summarizing what was intended to be accomplished), the Credits (references and other credits where due) and a Teacher Page (giving further details to teachers and which may also toggle other categories such as 'resources', 'standards' and so on).

Box 6.5

Check out the simplicity of the design of WebQuests at http://www.webquest.org/. The site offers examples of WebQuests for public perusal and introduces a simple authoring facility under the QuestGarden part of the site.

Tom March's list of Best WebQuests, found at http://www.BestWeb Quests.com, includes a collection of WebQuests linked in terms of their age level and subject matter. To see an example, visit the Schubert WebQuest at http://schubertquest.tripod.com/index.html and find out what happens when Schubert returns to earth, inhabits your body and you find both his unquenchable thirst to finish his music and his bad hair beginning to affect your life. You have no choice but to help him complete his unfinished pieces!

BLENDED LEARNING

Clearly none of these types of sophisticated e-Learning can form the exclusive basis of classroom activity, and the concept of 'blended learning' has grown up around the recognition that there will inevitably be a mix of e-Learning pedagogies and traditional/conventional pedagogies. However, to retain the benefits of both approaches any such blended course will require:

- students to see themselves as producers and not just consumers of information;
- a process of constructing knowledge and that this construction is a communal activity;
- students to be trained in the various technologies they are using, and particularly those needed to communicate or present to their peers;
- authentic coursework to be built in;
- presentation to peers to be a fundamental part of the communication activities, including placing it on the Web for use by students in subsequent years and for inspection by the wider community;
- active collaboration by all students in both the preparation and the presentation of the new knowledge and other outcomes for a shared and wider audience;
- use to be made of group work and project-based learning pedagogies;
- appropriate assessment techniques such as portfolios that may benefit the individual, their peers and the learners that follow them;
- resources to be presented in good time to enable pre-reading and optimum use of class time for communal discussion and group work;
- use to be made of peer tutoring and mentoring, with more experienced students taking on the role of mentor;
- students to take on responsibilities such as leading a discussion group; developing specific elements of course content.

As we have argued, e-Learning has the potential to allow students to become publishers and not just consumers of information through the use of tools ranging from the simple wordprocessor to Web and multimedia authoring tools. They can contribute to simple asynchronous discussions on email and bulletin boards, create their own weblogs or engage more synchronously with others in chat rooms. Such tools and environments enhance communication capabilities and cut across divisions of space and time. Digital audio, video, webcams and weblogs can capture and disseminate learning experiences for research and reflection. Databases, referencing packages, statistical and text analysis packages allow students the freedom to store, structure and analyse their own repositories of information and knowledge. Online tracking, monitoring software and adaptive learning environments assist in the structuring and analysis of their learning.

The communal constructivist approach requires that any e-Learning course should be dynamic and adaptive, and responsive to the community of learners. It must be recognized, therefore, that new activity will not emerge only in the disciplinary content of the learning. In a truly dynamic and adaptive course, in which students communally contribute to each other's learning, the method of delivery – the blending – will also inevitably be open to change.

7

Empowered Learners – Powerful Tools for Learning

ε-LEARNING TECHNOLOGIES

The ongoing information and communications technology revolution has often been compared to the advent of the printing press for the sheer magnitude of its actual and potential impact on society. The Internet represents a uniquely successful example of a massive sustained investment of creativity, innovation, time and money, which has revolutionized the individual's and society's ability to create, communicate and source information. Cast in the form of a learning environment, the accessibility to learners across the globe is virtually unrestricted. For example, while teaching a master's course at Trinity College, Dublin, one of us (Holmes) had the experience of mounting the course materials online in an open learning environment and found that a number of classes worldwide were enjoying the use of the materials; an instant audience that would not have been possible prior to the connectivity of the Internet and the linking of resources on the World Wide Web. It is not just that the Internet is huge, it also integrates many other technologies such as the telephone, radio and television. And it will continue to integrate them in ever more interesting ways.

Downloading movies is now commonplace and the prospect of designing tailor-made television channels with choices from various digital broadcasters is not far off being an everyday activity on the home computer.

There is now a range of technologies able to support the pedagogic models and instructional strategies that are the foundation of e-Learning. And so many new terms and concepts are beginning to emerge, for example 'ambient learning' and 'ubiquitous technologies'. Early e-Learning environments' such as the MOOs discussed in Chapter 1, were text-based, but are continuing to evolve in sophistication and functionality. An increasing proportion of tutors can publish learning materials on the Web and many will often use Web tools to add their own functionality. Increasingly, this moves the tutor closer to the role of developer and this process of examining 'what' is taught with 'how' it is taught is one of the fundamental changes that the integration of e-Learning will have on present teaching practice. Being a proficient programmer, of course, has its merits: 'The computer programmer ... is a creator of universes for which he alone is the law giver ... No playwright, no stage director, no emperor, however powerful, has exercised such absolute authority to arrange a stage or field of battle and to command such unswerving dutiful actors or troops' (Weizenbaum, 1984: 102). But few tutors will be able to master Web programming at the level Weizenbaum describes! Instead it is important to consider how tools can assist educators to provide students with the opportunity to develop higher-level skills. If the routine information dissemination that is characteristic of the majority of lecture-style teaching can be carried out by software, then the tutor can focus on scaffolding and supporting higher-order thinking skills, in addition to other enhancement activities such as co-ordinating online inputs from 'visiting' experts.

Sutton (1999) identifies four generations or iterations of the use of the technology in the change of focus in distance education, from its simplest form in which individual students engage in one-to-one dialogue with the tutor, to the most sophisticated system in which the tutor facilitates learning within a class group, members of which in turn collaborate with each other. The first generation is 'correspondence' teaching. Here text serves as the sole form of communication between student and tutor, usually by post but perhaps augmented by telephone tutorials. It would be rare in this mode to find much interaction between students who are taking the same course. The addition of media-based resources such as audio (radio) and video (television) in the second generation enhances the course content, but teaching methods and interaction remain largely the same. Third-generation distance learning focuses more on the electronic interaction and communication between the learners and the tutor, with both asynchronous and synchronous communications supporting the learning. Sutton's last stage is entitled the Education Object Economy (EOE). Here he points to the emergence of large-scale digital repositories of generic resources that can be used in a variety of systems, that is, resources that are interoperable and reusable. The tutor can literally 'pull them off the shelf', ready-made for building their own e-Learning systems. These can be either utilities (for example, drop-boxes for students to submit assignments electronically) or content (for example, a collection of worked examples in solving mathematical equations). The main focus to begin with is the transition between Sutton's second and third stage, the evolution of Internet-supported distance education and its basic ingredient, the Web page.

EARLY WEB PAGES – BASIC HTML

Anyone thinking of designing their own online learning space, even if they do not intend creating the website themselves, will find it useful to have some knowledge of the technologies involved in creating Web environments. Even a little knowledge of the technicalities will enable them to judge, to some extent, what is possible, and to work more effectively with a design team to set their ideas into practice. As mentioned in Chapter 3, the two key inventions underpinning the development of the World Wide Web were the Hyper Text Markup Language (HTML) and the uniform resource locator, developed in 1989 by Tim Berners-Lee.

Hyper Text Markup Language is the language that enables instructions to be given to a Web browser about how to read the text or other information it is required to display or use. The analogy of typing on a simple mechanical typewriter might help to conceptualize how HTML works. If underlined text is required, the typewriter must do it in two stages. The text must first be typed in full and then the type-head must be moved back to the beginning of it to enable the underline to be typed beneath it. When a manuscript was sent to the typist for typing, the person who created it would have underlined it on paper and the typist would understand this instruction.

Underlining, simple paragraph formatting and spacing were pretty much the limits of what you could do with text on a mechanical type-writer but printing presses offer much more variety. Copy editors, who check manuscripts or typescripts prior to printing as published books, newspapers columns and so on, 'mark up' the text with simple short hand codes that the typesetter understands. For a printing press this can be a wide range of formatting and stylistic features (colour, indentation, font changes, font sizes and so on) all marked up on the original script by the copy editor's short codes. When typewriting gave way to the quantum leap that was word-processing, a variety of text formatting, formerly only available to those who could access printing and typesetting facilities, became easy to achieve for the individual. They also had the facility of being able to edit and rework any mistakes on screen before committing to paper. Highlighting text on a wordprocessor is a simple matter of typing the text to be underlined and then selecting an 'underline' menu command or icon that automatically and instantly underlines it. Alternatively, selecting the underline facility first enables all subsequent text to be underlined until such times as the underline facility is 'turned off'. In either case, the wordprocessor simply activates an embedded 'underline' code, which is invisible on the screen unless it is specifically requested to be made visible.

The secret to HTML is to understand that it is an extension of this technique in which the display instructions are added to or embedded in the information (text or graphics) that is presented to the computer. Once browsers began to be written to interpret HTML, designers had an easy way to communicate instructions on complex screen information formats that the browsers would automatically execute. The embedded instructions generate displays and interactions that would previously have required separate programming. Today HTML and its extensions allow the Web designer to use a wide variety of eye-catching techniques for presenting information, and these are evident in many website front pages.

🖱 Box 7.1

Hyper Text Markup Language language is relatively simple in syntax and structure, with the codes for the actions placed within angle brackets: < >. Try a simple piece of HTML programming on a Windows-based personal computer. Open up an ordinary text editor like Notepad and type in:

<u>Please underline this sentence on the Web page<u>

Save the file as 'Testing HTML.html' in a convenient directory (or simply save it to the desktop) and close it. Now go to the directory in which it is saved (using Windows Explorer for example) and double-click on it. The browser window should open up with the text displayed as

<u>Please underline this sentence on the Web page</u>

It was the ability to embed links in HTML, seemingly such a small thing, that changed the way we disseminate information and encouraged the development of interactivity in electronic form.

Another innovation, which has been crucial to the development of the World Wide Web, is the URL or universal resource locator. A URL is the address of a Web page or website and enables computers to locate resources across the Internet. It essentially provides a pathway from one machine to another in the form of a protocol, which the browser interprets and uses to retrieve the appropriate file.

🖱 Box 7.2

Try to create your own Web page using an online HTML tutorial. Dave Kristula's popular HTML tutorial site (http://www.davesite.com/webstattion/html) provides a variety of tutorial and information support facilities for the beginner, including tutorials on how to write your own Web pages. The site provides information on how to get an

(Continued)

Internet provider, what HTML is and more advanced topics such as uploading, structuring and copyright. The site has an interactive section where you can type simple HTML code and then click the 'Check it Out!' button to see the effect. Dave argues that by learning HTML, the look and feel of Web pages can be more easily tailored.

Early Web pages took advantage of these two new inventions to link pages together and make connections between resources. The next development seems rather obvious today but was also hugely important – the cross-linking of indexes to an ever-growing resource base. Book indexes link topics to page numbers and, in a similar fashion, websites with embedded addresses to other sites was a new way of making connections or 'hyperlinks' between items of information. The ensuing growth in 'connectedness' was nothing short of exponential. Searching the Web initially involved finding pages of lists of sites which were related to the search query.

The first search engines began to appear in 1993/94 and at least three of them continue to this day: Lycos (http://www.lycos.com), AliWeb (http://www.aliweb.com) and WebCrawler (http://www.webcrawler.com). The analogy of a spider managing its web was captured in the names of Lycos, named after the wolf spider family, Lycosidae, and, more obviously, WebCrawler!

Box 7.3

WebCrawler has evolved into what is known as a 'meta-search engine', that is, it will search on a theme and/or genre of information across a variety of search engines including the market leaders, Google and Yahoo Search. Visit WebCrawler at http://www.webcrawler.com and search for 'Images' of James Joyce. Now try 'Audio' for an audio clip of Joyce reading from Ulysses, his most famous work. Finally, use the 'Video' meta-search to find a video clip of a Ulysses scene from Joseph Strick's 1967 film of the same name.

WebCrawler went 'live' on the Web on 20 April 1994 and their home page claims that by November of the same year they had 1 million search inquiries. The volume of searching across all engines is now almost innumerable. By August 2001, for example, the Google search engine tracked over 1.3 billion Web pages and by the end of 2004 this number had grown to just over 8 billion!

Early websites were generally text based and had few pages. They typically had a central 'homepage' with the address 'index.html' and links from that page. Initial Web design was all about presenting text in a catchy way and ensuring that the user's navigation around the site was as simple and consistent as possible. They were similar to electronic books or newspaper articles, with readers having to scroll down to see a full page. Too often they found themselves coming into a particular part of a site, to which a link had directed them, with little or no guidance as to where in the overall site they were. Clearly, designing for the Web had begun to outgrow the techniques that suited the traditional print medium.

Other problems, to which a print medium model gave rise in Web design related to the placing of text and graphics on a page. Just like a word-processor page, an HTML page is not very flexible when it comes to mixing text and graphics. Essentially, a graphic has to sit in the text in a box, otherwise various distortions of the graphic or text may arise. As Web design moved forward one solution was to lay out the pages using tables. This allowed the designer to ensure that empty spaces would be arranged above, beside and below text and graphics as appropriate. Tables also enabled people to think about 'what goes where?' on the Web page. Consider opening a book and then searching for the table of contents. Convention, developed over time, has placed the 'Contents' close to the beginning and most readers of any book will expect them to be there. Ultimately, links internal to a website began increasingly to be at the top or left-hand side of the screen in columns or rows and generally speaking that is where most people now expect to find them. Complex Web pages will, of course, have external access points on other parts of the screen also: top, bottom and right-hand side; and indeed anywhere that might catch the eye as necessary.

The use of a table framework also had other advantages. On the Web a designer has no control of the width of the browser window and originally there was a great deal of variation as monitors grew in size in tandem with advancing technologies. For graphic artists trained in print, it was a challenge to control the size and dimensions of aspects of their design. They sought to create their own designs in a fixed layout so that most Web browsers would present the page as the designer envisioned it. Here the idea was to use the table to create a restricted size in which to operate. This had the effect of making the website more like a piece of printed paper with clearly defined borders and margins. A user could open the site in most Web browsers on most monitors around the globe and still see the same thing. The size of screen would not matter as the pre-sized and restricted table would make sure the contents remained the correct size. Inside this main table-based page designers could place other smaller tables. The page might be thus divided into a number of separate sections with different information, with some sections being merged together to create navigation bars and so on. Although tables are no longer used to such a degree, the popular Web design package, Dreamweaver (http://www.macromedia.com), still uses them for layout.

🖱 Box 7.4

e-Learning websites increasingly depend on clear layout, navigation and expert graphic design. Familiarize yourself with a good style guide such as Patrick Lynch's and Sarah Horton's Web Style Guide at http://www.webstyleguide.com/. This comprehensive online text walks the budding designer through every stage from simple page design to multimedia strategies. Have a look also at the Bignosebird site, http://www.bignosebird.com/, where there are 'over 300 pages of [free] tutorials, reference materials and other free materials' for building interaction and functionality into your website. The Hot Potatoes site, web.uvic.ca/hrd/halfbaked/, includes free applications to enable the creation of interactive online exercises such as multiple-choice quizzes, jumbled-sentence puzzles and crosswords.

As websites began to front sophisticated and extensive commercial ventures (in selling, advertising or marketing online), their design became equally sophisticated and costly. Tools to support designing therefore range from simple wordprocessors, to powerful animation and graphics editors. Like the spelling and grammar checks on a wordprocessing package, an HTML editor can provide an automatic error check and help with structuring the layout of the text and so on. Many popular wordprocessing packages also have a 'Save as HTML' function but as many more types of people want to design their own simple websites, 'what you see is what you get', WYSIWYG editors, such as the free Web Weaver EZ at http://www.mcweb-software.com/wwez/, have begun to emerge. Typically, as in a wordprocessor, a menu bar is used to select text, highlight it with colour and add in hyperlinks or graphics.

THEN THERE WERE GRAPHICS

Earlier text-based websites were evolving from a focus on setting borders, margins and padding out cells to include a number of other considerations such as colour, contrast and layout, and how they harmonize to provide a focused site. e-Learning sites were evolving from being providers of content, to individualistic environments with their own specific feel or branding, an increasingly important feature for commercial e-Learning ventures. Graphics were thus the next big thing.

Mosaic was one of the first popular graphical Web browsers developed at the University of Illinois. The project was led by Marc Andreessen who went on to help develop the first commercially successful browser, Netscape Navigator. Microsoft eventually acquired the Mosaic code and went on to develop Internet Explorer. While Internet Explorer may be the most widely known browser, there are several other important systems including 'The fastest browser on Earth' (their words, not ours!) Opera 8 at http://www.opera.com/. Market Share's website at http://marketshare.hitslink.com/ provides usage data for the various browsers on a monthly basis and, for October 2005, these suggest approximately 87 per cent penetration for Internet Explorer, just over 1 per cent for Netscape, approximately 9 per cent for Firefox and just over 0.5 per cent for Opera 8.

As graphics became increasingly supported by browsers, and thus increasingly common, new opportunities for design emerged. The combination of high-powered Web browsers, the roll-out of broadband infrastructure and the use of graphics ultimately led to a quantum leap in the quality and innovativeness of Web design as graphic artists used all the tools at their disposal to move Web design up a notch.

The Web designer is a relatively new type of professional, often with skills that have evolved from painting, illustration or typography. Each of these disciplines contributes their own sense of balance, rhythm, contrast and proportion, and just as it would be in the traditional areas of landscape painting or magazine layout, the diversity in expression in Web design is exceptionally wide.

However, Web designers remain faced with a more restrictive environment than print or other 'manual' medium as they cannot control the user viewing experience, where this is governed by technical issues such as the digital colour palette or screen size available. Screen resolution continues to constrain the clarity of image presentation. Even the choice of font display, though hugely developed since the early days of teletype, remains relatively limited. If a designer wishes to create text with a font designed to be attractive to young children, they need to provide a font set that the browser can interpret and display. If they do not, the browser will fall back to a default substitute such as Times New Roman or Arial, with the design aspirations completely lost. The designer could still use their proprietary font but they would have to include each letter or word as an image thus increasing the processing and download times – other important factors to be taken into account when designing for the web.

One of the new opportunities offered by the Web, which can expand the impact of learning materials beyond any previously conceivable limits, is animation. Animated sequences can be used to attract the learner or other user by a range of features from something as simple as manipulation of screen objects to the complex near-to-video visuals of computer games and, of course, video itself. Learners will always find material presented in text form to be less engaging than that presented in video or video and text, and will likely assimilate and recall more information when it is supported by visuals. Thinking how to design information for this environment is therefore a matter of balancing the restrictions with the opportunities and not being afraid to push back the boundaries.

Liquid layout

Ultimately the Internet should have its own form and function rather than being limited to a layout more suited to the fixed print medium such as a magazine. As we have seen, tables originally acted as invisible design frameworks, which allowed for a locked-in control of the proportions of the site. However, the table format is clearly restrictive. Tables and nested tables remain very useful for news sites (see, for example, the columnar formats of the *Guardian* newspaper online at http://www.guardian.co.uk/ or the BBC News website at http://www.bbc.com/news/) but they are difficult to manage when any degree of complexity is involved. The upshot of the restrictions is that designers are being forced to spend large amounts of time adjusting and re-adjusting margins, and merging and dividing cells. In response to the growing need for flexibility a new solution, the liquid layout, emerged, in which the size of the browser window is immaterial as the Web page shrinks or expands to fit. Liquid layout is made possible through the use of 'cascading style sheets' (CSS), which define the look and feel of a site. Once defined the style sheet remains separate from the content but governs how it is presented. In a liquid layout, page displays are no longer fixed. Instead, the designer has to think of the variety of ways in which a user might wish to view the results of their work and must ensure that they can do so.

Another way of thinking about how content is created and presented for the Web is to take a role similar to that of a movie director. The script actions, text, dialogue, screen background, music, movement and animation all become the subjects of a 'storyboard', with the designer 'scripting' how each element is included or presented. Tools such as Macromedia Director (at http://www.macromedia.com) support such a way of looking at Web design and development. Another Macromedia product, Flash, has also made an impact by offering active control to every part of the design and enabling Web design features to be based on motion. The advanced facilities of allowing the learner to manipulate any animated clip themselves, for example to 'rewind' or view in slower motion, greatly assist them to assimilate the knowledge and information on offer. The result of these advances in technology and ease of creating animated sequences has been a huge rise in the use of multimedia for learning.

Box 7.5

To see examples of what is possible with Flash visit the website for the pop group Air's 1000 Hz Legend album: http://www.air-10000hzle gend.com/2.htm or the cartoon pop group Gorillaz website at http://www.gorillaz.com/intro.html.

Now have a go at a virtual adventure! An online site developed by the Library and Archives of Canada at http://www.collections canada.ca/education/art/05060211e.html features Flash-enriched activities that support problem-based learning. The site opens to tell you that help is needed to track down old Canadian paintings and prints dating from the 1800s from a little art shop in London. Off you go to Basil's Art and Antique Shop to put together your own collection of art that provides insight into early life in colonial Canada.

USABILITY

How users approach, navigate and generally experience a website is a growing area of interest and study called 'usability' and there is an increasing need to develop a body of knowledge relating to how Web designers create for optimization of education. Where elements of an e-Learning design might be used in several implementations, the key is to ensure that whoever might want them, can find and use them. Open-endedness and flexible combinations of text, graphics, video and audio therefore are the key stepping stones to enabling e-Learning design to become easier. Designers need to be the creators envisioned by Weizenbaum in the early 1980s, exploring with curiosity and supported by multidimensional ways of working with information. When outputs are sufficiently general in these applications, they are said to be 'interoperable', that is, they can be used in different e-Learning applications and environments. How they fit together might euphemistically be called 'shaken and perhaps stirred' to create new environments out of established ingredients; a bit like the different types of structure (house, church, office and so on) that can be made from the same building bricks. Many creative tools such as Adobe's Photoshop (at http://www.adobe.com) have up to 10 layers of 'undo' so that directions can be explored, examined and traced backwards to new points of departure. No creative canvas has ever been so pliable, no medium so flexible! Designing can be fun.

LEARNING OBJECTS AND REUSABILITY

The separation of content from presentation, achievable through cascading style sheet technologies, is the key to the new directions in Web design and has the power to impact on education at a fundamental level. Technology is increasingly making it easier to reshape digital content, taking into account the different needs of different learners. The reusability of presentation styles or content components is a parallel and equally important new direction for education. A potent rallying cry today for educational developers is to create 'learning objects' or modular e-content that can be used in different contexts – just like the bricks above, which can be used to build houses, churches or offices. These learning objects can be stored in electronic repositories for access by e-Learning developers as and when they need them.

Standards for interoperability

Encouraging the re-use of e-Learning components will ultimately save time and energy and lead to an overall improvement in the quality of material as tutors move beyond reinventing the wheel, each time they wish to commit some work to an e-Learning environment, into a more considered approach to design and delivery. The creation of large-scale free-to-access databases of e-Learning components or 'objects' would clearly result in reduced costs and increased flexibility for e-Learning designers and tutors alike, and several systems are emerging to assist in the process. An example of these is Burrokeet, which is an Open Source tool at http://www.burrokeet.org that takes existing content and assists in turning it into learning objects. To allow for learning objects to be used in different contexts, the objects must be created in specific 'interoperable' data formats. A number of initiatives exist to create such standards including SCORM, the Sharable Content Object Reference Model at http://www.adlnet.org. This format seeks to ensure that learning objects can be shared easily between different learning systems. However, as Gobee (2005) reminds us, learning objects cannot ever be free of context. In creating large-scale repositories of learning and teaching materials, therefore, additional consideration needs to be given to ways in which the individual tutor's 'touch' can be reflected in their own specific context.

Box 7.6

The open sharing of learning resources is becoming a very important dimension of e-Learning development and, in addition to standards initiatives like SCORM, there are a number of organizations that are developing accessible repositories of e-Learning objects. For example, visit 'The Inclusive Learning Exchange' (TILE) at http://www.barrier-free.ca/tile/, 'a revolutionary learning object repository service that responds to the individual needs of the learner'. Another is MERLOT (Multimedia Educational Resource for Learning and Online Teaching at http://taste.merlot.org/), which is free and designed for those teaching and learning in higher education. The repository is structured by discipline and nine categories of resources:

Case study	Collection	Reference material
Simulation	[of learning materials]	Tutorial
Drill and practice	Animation	Lecture/presentation
	Quiz/test	

A standard for profiling e-Learners – UKLeaP

Work is also progressing to ensure that common standards for transferring information about learners, throughout their life course, are available to e-Learning developers and users. The most important of these is the UK Lifelong Learner Information Profile (UKLeaP), which is due to be released as the British Standards Institute's BS8788. The 2003 announcement (http://www. imsglobal.org/pressreleases/pr03/006.cfm of the intention to create the standard give a flavour of its purpose:

'LIP [the Learner Information Profile] specifies a generic skeleton for information about learners' experience, capabilities, credentials and preferences. The UKLeaP profile will flesh out this general specification to provide a standard way of recording and exchanging UK specific information across the life long learning domain in the UK', said Ed Walker, CEO of IMS. ... The LIP specification and UKLeaP together are a complete solution for this vital component of e-Learning environments.

DIGITAL RIGHTS AND COPYRIGHT

Learning objects promise to deliver increasingly tailored courses but what about copyright? Appropriate re-use can only occur where authors of e-Learning materials are recognized for their efforts. Those wishing to use or customize the content must therefore respect the intellectual property rights of those who originally created the materials. With the facility of cutting and pasting quite seamlessly from any site, copyright is therefore a key issue on the Web. A number of potential problems exist and an initiative called Creative Commons at http://creativecommons.org/license/ allows authors to publish on the Web while setting out the uses they intend for their work. This might include telling site visitors that they will need the author's permission to use the material for commercial reasons or for deriving work from it. Creative Commons offers tools and tutorials to create licence information for any site, or to one of several free hosting services that have incorporated Creative Commons.

NEW DIRECTIONS – UBIQUITOUS TECHNOLOGY AND AMBIENT LEARNING

The future of e-Learning is opening up for everyone everywhere. Increasingly, mobile technology is allowing learning to move literally into the hands of the learners. In time this will change the ownership of the learning experience.

The moving of learning materials into learners' hands, in the sense of having it 'on their laptops', has clear implications for pedagogy. The impact of laptops and wireless applications in education will create a feeling in students of ownership of the materials and process. Search engine technologies ease the time-consuming burden of searching for information and thus free the learner to spend more time in applying the knowledge they are creating. Lightweight laptop and palmtop technology (including the combination of Internet-enabled telephones) puts the Web in the hands of learners anytime, anywhere (or at least where the learners can access a hard-wired or wireless portal!). The situation would appear to be relative to the ownership of the space in which the access is available. For example, in Becker's (2000) investigation of the educational uses of computers at more than 1,000 schools in Minnesota and California, classes that had access to computers in their classrooms used computers more extensively than if they had access to computer labs, even when there were many more computers in the lab. When wireless access is available to students, experience would also suggest that they use it more extensively than in circumstances in which they have to go to a specific location such as a workstation. The more the access space is the choice of the students, the more extensively they will use it.

🖱 Box 7.7

'Philadelphia's goal is to become the number one wireless city in the world and intends to set the standard by which wireless accessibility is measured. The city intends to enter into partnership with interested public and private parties to provide wireless access for the entire city.' Check out (at http://www.phila.gov/wireless/briefing.html) how much it will cost to make the Mayor of Philadelphia's ambitious plan to create a 135 square mile wireless (WIFI) zone to cover the entire city.

One of us (Holmes) has investigated this issue in a wireless environment project at Trinity College, Dublin. Wary of the words of Harvard's Frank Steen that 'every classroom can be a computer lab or a major distraction' (Steen, 2001: 1), the initiative involved rolling out a wireless network for students on master's and undergraduate courses in the computer science department. The students were encouraged to use their laptop computers within and outside classes as their primary learning tool. The potentially distracting effect of having students in a group session all linked to the Web through wireless access presents its own problems for tutors and its own solutions. Gay O'Callaghan, a key researcher on the project, likened some aspects of the project's processes to the children's story Pinocchio in her report entitled 'Cutting the strings in a wireless environment' (O'Callaghan, 2001). The Pinocchio effect is the worst case scenario when the tutor, rightly or wrongly, senses distraction rather than industry and asks the students to close their laptops! Just like Geppetto, who worried about how to control the results when he 'cut the strings' to give Pinocchio his freedom, some tutors will worry about empowering the students to do 'their own thing' and will retreat to the security of tradition and convention!

Though those who are less trammelled by such worries may argue that the students' freedom to choose how to engage with the technology should be the starting point (Geppetto should let go!), perhaps a better solution is to support students in using and, indeed, designing environments that they themselves prefer (Geppetto should be a guide-at-the-side). The best course seems to be a 'bit of both' – both sides committed to ensuring that the learning objectives are achieved, with students having freedom to choose and the tutors having a guidance role.

The team also recognized and reported the power of a communal constructivist environment in which all the students were enabled to create e-Learning tools for use by their peers. The students took part in a network that served as a dynamic space for both communication and production. Two important learning support tools developed by the students were a 'knowledge space' and an instant messaging facility. The knowledge space was a communally constructed digital repository which exploited the anytime, anywhere opportunities of the wireless environment with access to collections of documents, images, sounds, scientific data and software collated by the students. Instant messaging enabled tutor–student or student–student interactions (in any combination of one-to-one and one-to-many) when the appropriate people were online and the students had questions to ask or comments to make. Again Steen's observations were echoed as 'Dining rooms, libraries, lawns, athletics facilities, offices, hallways and classrooms become places for email, surfing the net, looking at course Web pages and instant messaging' (Steen, 2001: 1).

Each time new students connected to the network they extended it by becoming both producers and transmitters of new and unpredictable information, enabling them to adapt the college-wide connectivity according to their needs. What ultimately emerged was a dynamic space of collective subjectivities that enabled everyone to learn and contribute to everyone else's learning. The major driver for the successes in the project was the wireless mobility of anytime, anywhere – including during lectures and tutorials! With the witnessed increase of student engagement not just in this project but in many others around the world, it is not surprising that adoption of wireless in higher education is rapidly increasing. In their 2005 survey of over 500 US higher education institutions, the Campus Computing Project reported:

> the continuing expansion of wireless networks (WiFi) across all sectors of higher education. Almost two-thirds (64 percent) of campuses report strategic plans for wireless networks as of fall 2005, up from 55 percent in 2004, 45.4 percent in 2003, 34.7 percent in 2002 and 24.3 percent in 2001. More than a fourth (28.9 percent) indicate that full-campus wireless networks are up and running at their institutions as of fall 2005, compared to a fifth (19.8 percent) in 2004, 14.2 percent in 2003, and just 3.8 percent in 2000. Across all sectors, the 2005 data suggest that wireless services are available in more that two-fifths of college classrooms, up from a third (35.5 percent) in 2004. By sector, the proportion of wireless classroom ranges from 26.8 percent in community colleges (a gain from 24.8 percent last year) to 53.8 percent in private research universities (up from 47.4 percent in 2004. (CCP, 2005)

Instant messaging (IM) allows the user to know who else is available, that is, online, for them to contact immediately by email. Perhaps this is not always a good thing but the theory underlying it relates to the (dubious?) expectation that the person contacted will respond immediately. Certainly this is a communicative norm for a 'chat line' but in the context of work, and professional communications, replies and answers to questions may not be so immediately forthcoming, if only because the query may be complex. However, according to McDonald (2002):

> research firm Gartner has estimated that there are now more than 100 million instant messaging users worldwide, and that by 2005, IM will be used more often than e-mail. Gartner has also estimated that corporations using instant messaging could reduce internal e-mail volume by 30 to 40 percent, and voice mail volume by 10 to 15 percent.

Perhaps if the culture demands and facilitates instant messaging, such savings will be possible.

Mobile wireless communications and their associated applications have become the norm for interaction in the business community and among young people in general. The otherwise distractive effect of multiple simultaneous interactive communications can instead be productively channelled into the creation and development of dynamic learning environments, which empower both student and tutor. The cultural lag between the use of 'no strings' communications 'on the street' and their adoption within traditional learning environments may be avoided by inviting the imaginative contributions of young people, which exploit the potential inherent in the wireless environment and enable Pinocchio to realize full liberation.

Despite the plethora of applications and supporting technologies mentioned above, the fact remains that e-Learning is still in its infancy. The 'killer application' has not yet surfaced and e-Learning is still very often an add-on to existing practice in much the same way as the first television shows were filmed radio performances. Although a network in name and geographic spread, the Internet is a dynamic creation of the computer, not the traditional network of the telephone or television industry. But the signs of change are apparent and it is now providing such new services as transmission of real-time audio and video streams. Its very pervasiveness coupled with mobile computing and communications is underpinning the new paradigm of anywhere, anytime e-Learning.

Among the emerging new services, perhaps the most important is Internet telephony, which promises very quickly to revolutionize voice communications, primarily through much reduced costs to the consumer. As mentioned in Chapter 2 (*Economist*, 2005), it is more a question of 'when?' than 'if?'. The major telecoms companies are currently engaged in a commercial war against fledgling voice over Internet protocol (VOIP) companies and, if current cost differentials are anything to go by, the winners will clearly be the users (see, for example, the call charges of Telediscount at www.telediscount.co.uk). Quite soon it is expected that television services, exploiting satellite and full digital broadcasting, will also be cheaply and efficiently offered over the Interenet. 'Narrowcasting' will become easier and will exploit the existence of so many same-interest groups already on the Internet by enabling specific (that is, narrow) broadcasts to be created and delivered (anytime, anywhere!) to them. The economic exploitation, no more and no less than its exploitation for learning, will likely be comprehensive, rapid and diverse; and there will undoubtedly be more booms and busts to add spice to the enrepreneurial scramble. How the Internet, and our usage of it, will shape up as these developing services become more sophisticated, remains to be seen.

Central to this vision of an Internet-dominated future, however, has to be the availability of the new technologies to all citizens in all nations – among whose number we include those who have been or have the potential to be excluded from education because of economic disadvantage, geographic isolation or physical impairment. Giving these people the freedom of the Internet is the focus of the next chapter.

e-Learning – Learner Emancipation

e-Learning and accessibility are the key themes of this chapter, which explores the impact of e-Learning on communities of learners who have special challenges or experience special access difficulties. The specific focus is on the visually impaired community as they are arguably the most empowered when information is accessible and one of the most 'locked out' when it is not. Making e-Learning environments maximally accessible to visually impaired people is one of the main challenges facing e-Learning designers and tutors.

Building knowledge is an essential part of every individual's learning in the twenty-first century. Everyone should have the opportunity to be part of this process and when it happens in a social context they should always be valued for their contribution. However working against the integration of all members of society, both in the school and university and in the workplace, is the emerging 'digital divide'. Those without access or without the assistive technologies that can enable their access, can fall behind or indeed may never get started, in terms of education or opportunities in the workplace. e-Learning can help to counteract disadvantage, but only when it is accessible itself! One example that shows the potential reach of assistive technologies across the divide is the Indian e-Learning centre for the blind, which first opened its doors in 2003. It has been estimated by the National Council of Education Research and Training in New Delhi, that the centre has the potential to bring distance education to over 2 million blind children (World of Science, 2003).

> ### ⌐🖱 Box 8.1
>
> Everyone can do their bit to address the digital divide, in whatever form it takes. Why not visit the Digital Divide Network at http://www.digitaldividenetwork.org, which describes itself as the Internet's largest community for educators, activists, policy-makers and concerned citizens. Take part in working to bridge the digital divide by sharing documents, publishing a blog, taking part in discussions with colleagues and, even, building your own online community.

Disabilities of all kinds are relatively common in the older age ranges of the population, a section of society that continues to grow as health care improves and mortality rates fall. The European Union (EU) estimates that as the number of elderly people will continue to grow as a percentage of the total population, 37 per cent of the population will be over 60 years of age by the year 2050 (EU, 2006). There will be a significant increase is in the 80+ age band where disability is most prevalent and one of the most disabling conditions is deterioration or loss of sight. The potential, then, is for a growing digital divide in the area of able and disabled citizens, almost irrespective of whether the disabled person has high information and communications technology competence and convenient, low-cost access to that technology. If it is not made accessible through assistive technologies it could be a technological white elephant for them.

Disabled members of rural communities are often unable to participate fully in employment without moving to larger urban centres, perhaps leaving their families on whom they may otherwise depend for day-to-day support. e-business opportunities not only allow them to become valuable participants in the workforce from their own home or locality, but also allow disabled people to develop skills that can be shared within their own local communities. Indeed, they may become local employers if the business context allows.

Perhaps the success of society should be judged on the opportunities it offers for its weakest members, and in this respect e-Learning certainly fosters collective learning in an inclusive manner. Technology can help 'normal' people to do special things but, equally, special people can be helped to achieve success in 'normal' activities that would be otherwise beyond them. In the same manner that assistive technologies such as wheelchairs, hearing aids or walking canes can support people with physical impairments to achieve more in their lives, information and communication technologies can open up new ways to enhance the lives of disabled people. However, e-Learning can only emancipate disabled or other disadvantaged learners if it is designed to cater for all possible learners.

There is, therefore, an increasing recognition of the need to design for universal access so that a wide variety of learners has the opportunity to learn in online environments. However, there needs also to be recognition of the importance of social issues. Warschauer (2003) argues that addressing the digital divide is not simply a matter of connecting people to the Internet but includes social aspects such as political, economic and linguistic factors that inhibit access or usage. Such factors are key to understanding and influencing the development of e-Learning as a field, in a context in which much of the world's population is on the wrong side of the divide with reduced or non-existent opportunities to participate in and benefit from the information age. These factors need to be addressed alongside technical issues of access to software and hardware (Warschauer, 2003).

ASSISTIVE TECHNOLOGY ISSUES AND OPPORTUNITIES

Visually impaired learners are taught to read using Braille texts (that is, the printed text has each letter of the words represented by a pattern of raised dots on the paper instead of inked letters). Learning Braille is key to accessing information but when study texts are not available in Braille or as audio recordings, as might be the case in universities where courses often evolve year on year, students need assistance from note-takers and student support providers. e-Learning can make a difference here by affording students with visual impairments equal opportunities to access the necessary information – anywhere, anytime.

Using a screen-reader package, a visually impaired student can open Web pages and have a synthetic voice read the on-screen text to them. There are a number of speech output packages that can be used this way including JAWS (http://www.freedomscientific.com/) and the combined screen magnifier, reader and Braille system, Supernova (http://www.dolphincomputer-access.com/). When such software is expensive it can seriously hinder access for the most needy and so new and more effective ways of delivering 'speaking' screens are constantly being explored. Technologies such as Voice eXtensible Mark-up Language (VXML), in which the Web pages have the option of speech built in, may hold the answer. Voice eXtensible Mark-up Language allows for user interfaces that support voice input through automatic speech recognition (ASR), and voice output through text-to-speech synthesis (TTS). An indication of its importance is shown by the fact the VoiceXML Forum at http://www.voicexml.org/overview.html comprises several key Internet and communications companies such as AT&T, IBM, Lucent and Motorola.

Torres et al. (2002) have reported on the use of a number of different possibilities for developing voice online as part of their VISUAL (Voice for Information Society Universal Access and Learning) project. They concluded that VXML was superior to a variety of other techniques. They argue that VXML should be considered Web navigation's third dimension because, quite simply, if an approach makes websites more natural and attractive for visually impaired people, then it will equally improve the interaction for sighted persons.

Other important assistive technologies include screen magnifiers (for example, Zoomtext at http://www.aisquared.com/index.cfm) and Braille outputs (for example, Duxbury at http://www.duxburysystems.com/). Some operating systems, such as Apple's Mac OS X Tiger, have accessibility features built in. The Mac VoiceOver interface (http://www.apple.com/macosx/features/voiceover/) allows for magnification options, keyboard control and 'speaking' the contents of files and reporting onscreen activity. By assigning unique voices to different types of information, users can quickly distinguish information sources. Voices can also be tailored by adjusting pitch, speech rate and volume.

Having such access to information and communication facilities, on a par with their sighted peers, is important for learners with visual impairments but Nielsen (2001) estimates that it still takes such users three times longer to access information on the Internet than their full-sighted peers. Nielsen's study observed 84 vision-impaired users and 20 sighted peers as they performed a variety of tasks, including finding information online and comparing and contrasting resources across 19 websites in the USA and Japan. Nielsen concluded that more thought was needed at the beginning of the design process to implement higher usability levels, which would then ensure more success in tasks, faster completion, fewer errors and greater satisfaction with the sites.

⌐🖰 Box 8.2

You can test any website for usability with Bobby™. Choose a website and enter its URL into WebXACT at http://webxact.watchfire.com/ to test the Web pages on three factors: quality, accessibility and issues of privacy. 'Bobby' is provided by Watchfire as a testing tool to help identify barriers to accessibility and so make it easier for Web designers and developers to comply with existing accessibility guidelines, including the USA's Section 508 of the Rehabilitation Act. Examples of the accessibility requirements on which Bobby will report include readability by screen readers, alternative text equivalents for images, animated elements and video displays.

DESIGNING FOR ACCESSIBILITY

As new learning opportunities are hosted on the Internet, students with special difficulties need to be taken into account. The training needs of people who learn differently can be overlooked when organizations provide online training for their employees or students. Very often tutors simply may not know or understand what is needed to make the e-Learning environment easier for all students.

People who are visually impaired have a range of needs when it comes to accessing information. Some people with low vision can read large print with the help of screen magnification, while others may have limiting conditions such as 'tunnel vision' and may be able to read a single line at a time but not be able to scan up and down a page of text. Some visually impaired people may have become blind after years of being able to see and may need at least some of the context of the text explained to help them assimilate the material through the use of their pre-knowledge. Others may be blind from birth and be less interested in what things look like. Instead, they will have their own internal representations and will likely focus more on simply accessing the information.

As technology evolves it tends to become less rather than more accessible. Early emails with their direct and simple text-based communication made it relatively easy for visually impaired people to communicate. As interfaces and applications became more graphically oriented, emails began to be sent using HTML with visually attractive embellishments such as colour, background patterns and perhaps animated icons. Visual attraction is in the eye of the beholder, of course, and in circumstances in which screen contrast is made appealingly subtle, a weakly sighted person may find it a strain to read or simply unreadable. The mild but widely distributed disability of 'colour blindness' is a more obvious candidate for causing screen problems for a large proportion of the population. The evolution of Web screen presentation from text to nested tables was very confusing for those using screen readers that read across the tables rather than within each individual table. These evolving Web pages, though meant to be scanned quickly, varied considerably in how content featured in their structure. For example, key facts and figures might be found in the centre of one page and on the bottom right-hand corner of another. This, of course, meant that screen readers could take a long time to locate appropriate information, and might often be unsuccessful. Having links and navigation devices in different places on pages also served as a hindrance because visually impaired users were unable to find a pattern. As nested tables gave way to animated graphics, matters became much worse. Flash-based Web pages, opening with swirling letters emerging to form the name of the course for example, may be aesthetically pleasing to many students but may leave a visually impaired student and their screen-reading package, very lost.

> ### 🖱 Box 8.3
>
> There are many applications for text to audio, such as listening to Web pages when carrying out activities or putting into practice a series of instructions from a help menu for example. Test a few pages of your choice using ReadPlease, a free text-to-speech program that highlights each word as it is being read. You can download the software and voices for the program from the following website: http://www.read please.com.

Technically it is not difficult to create HTML Web pages in a manner that makes them accessible, but animated, interactive and multimedia materials are much more troublesome. Many software houses are now more aware of the issues but, for some, accessibility is still merely the provision of an alternative text-only version (though that at least is a start!). The Techdis website (at http://www.techdis.ac.uk/index.php?p=1_3) offers advice on what should be considered from the beginning of the design process. This advice covers ease of navigation, help for searching and easy to follow content layout and text descriptions ('alt' text) for images. At a level below the screen presentation issues, the advice is to ensure that the coding of the site should be provided in an accessible manner including descriptions of forms and tables.

Designing for accessibility is important if e-Learning is to help disabled students realize their promise and become independent learners. As some would undoubtedly argue, accessible e-Learning environments have larger markets because they have more learners to choose from. The evolution of technology, both software and hardware, has often resulted in a focus on visualization, such as ensuring the mouse pointer appears at the screen position at which the user wishes to be. 'Universal Design' or 'Design for All' initiatives extend the concept and seek to support the largest possible target audience, including those users who are, for example, deaf or have motor function difficulties. The promotion of an inclusive mind-set for designers is therefore a major part of the remit of the World Wide Web

Consortium's Web Accessibility Initiative (see http://www.w3.org/WAI/). The WAI is dedicated to creating guides, strategies and information on how to make the Web more accessible to all. It seeks to examine the issue of open access from as many perspectives as possible, and their research includes coverage of the following components:

- information developers and their tools
- content: both the information and the markup code
- interfaces such as assistive technologies, including screen readers and magnifiers
- user experience: including usage patterns and strategies.

EVALUATION OF ASSISTIVE TECHNOLOGIES

According to Edyburn (2000b) Web designers and users have only recently begun to consider the issues of assessment in using assistive technologies. Several sources are helpful in this regard. For example, Watts et al. (2004) have reviewed alternative models of assessment that are inclusive for students with disabilities. They state that it is important to provide periodic reviews of the appropriateness of the technology for the students as students' needs may not be similar. Chambers's Consideration Model (1997), for example, stresses the need for periodic review procedures and ongoing consideration of how the assistive technology performs. Models that take multiple perspectives of the learner's activities, such as Zabala's (2002) guide for considering assistive technology, examine not only the student engagement with the technology but also the environment, tasks and tools. Only when e-Learning software is designed to be flexible in terms of a learner's preferred learning style, abilities, disabilities, needs and goals over a period of time, can the assistive technology be considered to be performing appropriately.

INTERNATIONAL INITIATIVES IN ACCESSIBILITY

As the development, design and use of the Internet becomes more an integral part of society, standards bodies are emerging and promoting interoperability and increasingly accessibility. There are three European Standardization

Organizations (ESOs – at http://www.eeurope-standards.org) 'which share responsibility within Europe for creating standards, each within its own designated technical area: European Standardization Committee (CEN), European Electrotechnical Standardization Committee, (CENELEC) and European Telecommunication Standards Institute (ETSI)'. The standards take the form of workshop agreements, such as CEN Workshop Agreements developed under the eEurope Action Plan in the European Union. They are available online free of charge from the CEN/ISSS Web pages at http://www. cenorm.be/isss.

In 1999, the European Commission (EC) launched its eEurope 2002 – An Information Society for All initiative. The action plan set out to accelerate equality of access as well as promote computer literacy. A key part of this process was to foster communication and co-operation between the end users and the providers. The Action Plan for eEurope 2005 (EU, 2002) followed on from the ending of eEurope 2002 and was designed to build on the initial successes by promoting new services and jobs, thereby contributing to the further modernization of society and boosting productivity. Again part of the initiative stressed the importance of all European citizens being able to participate in the global information society. The Action Plan views social cohesion as a key step in moving the EU towards a competitive, knowledge-based economy by 2010.

🖱 Box 8.4

Check out the 'i2010' initiative (European Information Society in 2010) at http://europa.eu.int/information_society/eeurope/i2010/index_en.htm, which aims to ensure an integrated approach to information society policies in Europe. It builds on the eEurope 2005 Action Plan (see http://europa.eu.int/information_society/eeurope/2005/all_about/action_plan/index_en.htm) and encompasses the promotion of cultural diversity in addition to regulation and research.

In the USA accessibility is supported by legislation. In 1986 the Americans with Disabilities Act was drafted and approved, and has had a powerful impact in guaranteeing equal opportunity for all in terms of access to goods and services, and participating in employment and the community life. There is debate in the USA as to how far the Americans with Disabilities Act (ADA) should be extended into the 'cyberspace' of the Internet. The Act states that businesses should provide easy access for disabled people but the Internet has not yet been legally interpreted as a place of public access. The rulings to date are not encouraging and the predominant view is that although accessibility is an important goal, it cannot be forced on all websites (Short, 2003). The US government, however, has taken the important initial step of requiring that federal and agency websites provide access to the disabled.

In relation to e-Learning specifically, the US Individuals with Disabilities Education Act Amendments of 1997 held that assistive technology was a key aspect of an Individualized Education Program (IEP) team's planning process for children receiving special education services (Edyburn, 2000a). In the past 10 years such technologies have included personal computers, communication devices, switches and specialized keyboards (Blackhurst and Edyburn, 2001). Federal law (Individuals with Disabilities Education Act, 1997) and assessment literature (Edyburn, 2000b; Haines and Sanche, 2000; Johnson and Johnson, 2002; McLoughlin and Lewis, 2001) clearly indicate a mandate for the inclusion of a variety of people to make educational decisions with and on the behalf of students with disabilities. Hager and Smith (2003) believe that the US Congress intends that assistive technologies should create new opportunities for learners with disabilities to participate in education. In the future, therefore, e-Learning may well be part of streamlined, individualized personal planning for students with special needs.

e-Learning may thus assist schools in delivering a curriculum that supports equal access. However, the international trends towards integration of students with special needs into mainstream school systems can result in considerable pressure being placed on teachers to meet the specific individual needs of students but without the necessary training. Specific courses for educators, access to regulations and information for schools and parents, and specially adapted materials for students will all assist in creating specialized adaptive learning environments, but much remains to be done to make for smoother integration.

One initiative, the Social Assistance for/with the Visually Impaired (SAVI) project funded by the European Union (details at http://www.formatex.org/micte2005/241.pdf), currently seeks to address this need through creating a partnership involving researchers from the UK, Ireland, Portugal, Greece and the Czech Republic. Of these, only the UK to date has used an online model of delivery for training teachers of the visually impaired. Teachers of the visually impaired need to understand and avail themselves of the latest assistive technology. For this reason the SAVI environment is designed to support online course delivery and online community building using the same tools as the target students of the teachers involved.

BUILDING A SUPPORTING COMMUNITY NETWORK

A theme running through the book is the creation of communities of learners, working on communal constructivist principles. As outlined earlier, this means that it is not only learning from each other but creating a learning environment that sustains itself through the use of existing learners' inputs to support new learners, and to contribute to the learning of existing members. In the case of visually impaired learners, Lynch et al. (2005) puts a positive spin on the old cynical jibe by promoting a model of the blind leading the blind. This model draws on the social model of disability (Barnes, 1991; Finkelstein, 1992; Oliver, 1990; 1996) in which vision-impaired people are encouraged to draw on their learning experiences and create a more balanced relationship between themselves and non-disabled people. Communication with other visually impaired people, based on email lists that are created and supported by people with disabilities, connect people who have very unique questions with others who may have the answers.

One such community is the Visually-Impaired Computer Society of Ireland (VICS – at http://www.vics-ireland.org/), which was established in 1986 by a number of blind and visually impaired computer programmers to assist blind and visually impaired computer users. The specific aims of the community are to support new users, to inform and encourage employers, to encourage software developers to produce outputs that are more accessible and to assist those who wish to make electronic activities more accessible. The VICS has since grown to become a nationwide initiative and is a good example of how a simple tool, such as an email list, can be used to include the blind and partially sighted in a greater variety of decision-making and development activities.

When supporting a 'blind leading the blind' model of e-Learning, it is clearly a key requirement to ensure that learners can easily avail themselves of the support of their peers. Such a communal approach must be at the heart of the provision and will contribute considerably to the success of their present learning and that in the future. The creation of communally 'owned' learning objects becomes a multi-vocal process whereby members of the community contribute the diversity of their thinking and ideas to the creation of materials and teaching resources. This process was successfully followed in a project conducted by one of us (Holmes). The project, entitled the Accessible Communities for E-Business (ACE at http://www.inishnet.ie) brought together a group of vision-impaired adults to experience the development and testing of an e-community where they could collaborate to build the skills necessary to take part in and contribute to the changing workforce. The participants, who were drawn from both urban and rural locations, were also invited to contribute to the development of materials for future generations of learners. The initiative achieved its aim of increasing vision-impaired people's access to e-Learning and skills development with tailor-made courses such as modules for JAWS users in the European Computer Driving Licence (ECDL, 2006) programme.

Box 8.5

Check out the ECDL for People with Disabilities (ECDLPD) project at http://ecdl-pd.aib.uni-linz.ac.at/What_ECDLPD_is.html. This project seeks to promote vocational integration of people with disabilities by exploring ways that they can demonstrate levels of computer skills and how best the employers, trainers and the public can support their integration. The European Computer Driving Licence has provided people across Europe, and increasingly internationally, with a way of recognizing a standard set of computer skills. It sets out to provide an international standard certification that covers skill areas such as file management, creating, saving and merging documents, and Internet and email skills. Employers find it easy to determine the level of skill a potential employee has if they have ECDL qualifications and as a result many large employers, such as hospital trusts in the UK, are implementing the ECDL at work.

The ACE participants became more empowered learners as their engagement in the e-community improved their technological skills through contact with their peers and e-mentors in a twinning process. As their skills improved, the participants were in turn encouraged to 'twin' as mentors for new members to the site. They were also encouraged to add to the knowledge base and to contribute to the sharing of new knowledge by creating course materials from their own inputs. To encourage ease of creation of new materials the Accessible Communities for E-Business project website also incorporated audio files; a feature that facilitated more authentic and accessible presentation of information than a screen reader's synthesized voice.

Box 8.6

One way to make multimedia files accessible to the visually impaired is through Audio Description. Audio description offers a 'voice-over' on any form of visual information including videos or multimedia presentations. In a computer screen context, the narration that the blind or partially sighted person hears describes the actions and changes on the screen, reads the screen prompts and any other functional information. Check out the technique on the University of Washington website, http://www.washington.edu/accessit/articles?79.

From the beginning of the project, the participants were consulted at every stage in order to create an environment in which participants and developers worked as equal partners. Ultimately this communal and collegial process has been commended by the Irish government (NCBI, 2003: 3).

Such initiatives have the potential to impact considerably on the lives of people who are often disenfranchised by having a very restricted engagement with an increasingly complex information society. Being able to do things for themselves is an intrinsic and powerful motivation for those who are physically or intellectually impaired, and participants in the Accessible Communities for E-Business project have testified to a more positive outlook on their own computer abilities and their confidence to seek new employment. Not only did the participants benefit from e-Learning, they also saw how an e-community can grow and ultimately provide opportunities for vision-impaired people who wish to take further e-Learning courses and achieve higher qualifications. The e-community helped to demystify the concept of e-Learning for them and provided an environment that promoted their knowledge-building activities within a carefully conceived online environment.

Technology can help ordinary people do special things and, as we have argued here, it can also assist special people to do ordinary things. The best possible future for people with disabilities in Europe is to be as much a part of ordinary life as possible. There has been a widespread move to 'mainstream' students with special needs in school and university classrooms, yet this has meant that the tutors involved may not have the skills they need to best support them. The SAVI project team is studying ways forward, within the European context, for educators who will be teaching visually impaired students, and who are looking for information and experiences that can help them deliver a more accessible national curriculum to meet their needs more effectively.

e-Learning – Endless Development?

While deriving its underpinning theories from such notable scholars as Plato, Rousseau, Skinner, Dewey, Vygotsky and Piaget, to name but a few, e-Learning is arguably eclipsing their impacts as the most dynamic development in education ever. Even with several decades already behind us, there seems no end to the innovation and development that stretches into the future for e-Learning. For now and the foreseeable future, e-Learning remains 'mission critical'. It has emerged as an unparalleled explosion of innovations, creating opportunities for enriched experiences in traditional education and for enhancing the breadth of opportunity and content for lifelong learning. The scope for e-Learning's future development is so wide that it is with some trepidation that we attempt to paint a picture of the future.

Structuring a 'look' into the future, then, is a daunting task but it is helpful to consider it in terms of the two themes that have dominated this book, that is, the social and technological dimensions of e-Learning. The emerging trends in these themes may be discussed under a variety of headings but prominent among them are:

- e-Learning as change catalyst;
- improved learner-aware designs;
- blending the old, the new and the previously impractical;
- the challenges of assessment for e-Learning;

- making communal learning accessible;
- rights and entitlements across the digital divide;
- new convergences.

THE EDUCATION SYSTEM AND CHANGE

Larry Cuban sums up the current situation on the integration of computers in education as 'oversold and underused' (Cuban, 2000). And instances of computers metaphorically or otherwise 'remaining in their boxes', that is, delivered to a school or college but lingering underused as wordprocessors, or unused as storeroom clutter, are more common than we might care to admit. However, change can be a grindingly inexorable process and several major drivers are persistently pushing the e-Learning message across the world.

One of these drivers is based on the political and economic argument that each nation needs to be competitive in the global marketplace and that the development of information and communications technology capacity is the key stimulant. The pursuit of this goal has long gripped Western countries and it is now being taken up with alacrity in developing nations. As the US-based World Information Technology and Services Alliance (WITSA) president, Harris Miller observes: 'Spearheaded by India and its successful entry into the software development market, other countries are following its lead in droves. The resulting competition has energized politicians at both ends of the spectrum as the developed countries fight to grow the jobs of their local constituents' (WITSA, 2004). As an example of the attention now being brought to bear in addressing the information and communications technologies capacities of the developing nations, WITSA figures show that one of the poorest nations in the world, Bangladesh, is currently spending the least money per capita on information and communications technologies at only US$11 per capita, compared to a US$4,147 projected for the USA. However, in comparison with the lowest worldwide projected growth rate (6.7 per cent) of the already well-resourced North American region, Bangladesh's growth rate in information and communications technologies spending is expected to top 20 per cent, the highest rate anywhere. On a global basis, the WITSA projections show that information and communications technologies spending, which peaked at 7.4 per cent of global total spending in 2000, will settle at around 6.9 per cent through to 2007.

Such levels of investment need skilled employees and users to give a good return. A proportion of these will inevitably be 'journeyman' operatives (for example, involved in keyboarding data) and users (for example, engaged in Web browsing), but the greater the proportion of people with skills to 'add value' to the knowledge and usage system, the more likely the technology will enhance the economy with innovative products and processes. The arguments are both simple and plausible. In a global marketplace, for such is today's consumer base, the sellers of goods or services need their product to be 'visible' to those who have a need for it and to be marketed to those who might need it. Traditionally this visibility (marketing or advertising by any other name) has been achieved nationally at best, but often only locally, through the media (television, radio and newspapers), billboards and mail shots. But the Web has changed that. In a rapidly burgeoning level of information and communications technologies penetration, the Web currently reaches 85 million users in China alone. Not every enterprise can have a product that will sell in numbers in China, but if they do have a globally attractive product, the world is truly their 'oyster' of selling opportunities. Yet the truth is that no budding entrepreneur, advertising executive or marketing manager is born with Web design skills. No prospective purchaser is born with browsing and criterion-based searching skills, never mind simple keyboarding and emailing skills.

Each nation's education system (schools, colleges, universities and training organizations) is therefore being forced to sit up and deliver the full gamut of information and communications technology skills, from basic literacy skills to sophisticated applications for Web design, economic modelling, design engineering and so on. Hardly a part of society's existing knowledge base escapes the wind of change that information and communications technology developments bring. Having underused computer resources will increasingly become unforgivable. e-Learning will, in turn, become a major part of information and communications technologies education and training, in school and college contexts, and in university courses and work-based learning environments. But the story of e-Learning's future roles does not stop there.

e-Learning is a transformative technology. It has the capability of catalysing major changes in education and indeed society more generally. For example, questions have to be asked about the modern-day effectiveness and relevance of the traditional school. Existing patterns of restricted arrangements for learning in the UK – for example, the ubiquitous 9.00 a.m. to 3.30 p.m. school day, the compartmentalized timetables in which a student may get as little as a 40-minute daily ration of mathematics, the general lack of inter-disciplinarity in learning as the rigid curriculum enables subjects to maintain their disciplinary boundaries (separate English, history, science, and so on) and the intensive testing regimes imposed by government, which deflect students from learning – are increasingly being recognized as inadequate and inappropriate to the needs of today's learners. Enter e-Learning, a mode of learning that can be accessed anytime, anywhere, if the hardware and Internet access is available. Just as important as it is proving to be in the traditional education sectors, e-Learning is providing a huge fillip to lifelong learning. Whether in the workplace or the community, e-Learning opens up the realm of education to everyone and, most importantly, to those who would otherwise face disadvantage or simply lack of opportunity. It is a much more inclusive mode of education than the traditional school–(college)–university environments, so much so that one of the main objectives in the European Union's eEurope 2005 programme was to make educational institutions more open to all learners:

> All schools and universities, as well as other institutions that play a key role in e-Learning (museums, libraries, archives), should have broadband Internet access for educational and research purposes by end 2005 ... All universities should offer online access for students and researchers to maximise the quality and efficiency of learning processes and activities by end 2005. (eEurope, 2005)

e-Learning also has the potential to change practices and conventions considerably. For example, the growth of learning communities, with either a specific focus (for example, self-help groups with specific illnesses as their focus) or a more general purpose (for example, supporting modern language teachers), accentuates the natural collaborative nature of much successful learning. Such groups may previously have corresponded in a relatively restricted manner (for example, by post and perhaps with meetings where practical), but the Web, with dedicated websites, chat rooms and blogs, can literally transform collaborative activities into live or next-to-live interactions. Online work-based learning can bring external experts into the workplace and can generate internal mentor–mentee systems that efficiently dovetail with normal working.

The catalytic effect of e-Learning, which promotes change in the traditional environment, is underpinned by several key features which usually appear in some form or other in its main manifestations:

- its inclusiveness of all kinds of learners;
- the diversity of its content;
- the diversity of learning goals it can support;
- its capacity to provide individualized education programmes;
- its increasing sophistication in function, complemented by its increasing ease of use;
- its anywhere, anytime flexibility.

Perhaps its most important feature, however, is the manner in which the individualization is actually a central element of its communal approach, that is, the individual learner is supported in a learning community. Traditional learning environments can deliver many of these features up to a point, but arguably rarely does. However, e-Learning is likely to increase the expectations of learners to new levels of individualization, ready access to knowledge and inclusive social contexts.

IMPROVED LEARNER-AWARE DESIGNS

e-Learning systems are set to become evermore learner-aware with significant innovations and improvements in physical user interfaces and the software that runs them. Adaptive technologies, which 'learn' the user's individual characteristics, are vitally important for many users, sometimes for convenience and sometimes as a necessity. For example, voice and writing recognition are becoming more sophisticated, driven largely by the needs of professionals such as doctors, dentists and lawyers. The need is age-old. Notes from clinical examinations have to be recorded, accurately transcribed and stored; all time-consuming processes. An effective voice or writing recognition system is a major boon to busy professionals. The side-benefits for other users are also very important. With better voice or writing recognition systems, more opportunities are opened up for disabled users who cannot otherwise easily participate in an e-Learning environment via the keyboard. Complementary to recognition facilities are screen-reading systems. While perhaps not benefiting from the commercial drive to cater for doctors and lawyers, these are also becoming more sophisticated and accurate, again enabling many otherwise excluded users to avail themselves of e-Learning opportunities.

Developments in haptic devices for e-Learning are also gathering pace. Haptic devices enable users to 'feel' the results of their inputs through an interface that mediates their touch. Graphic artists and designers can, for example, 'feel' texture in their designs through the small forces that the haptic pen or brush feeds back to their hands. Improvements in the accuracy and sensitivity of the various joysticks, roller balls and pens are giving new meaning to the interaction that physically impaired people can experience in virtual worlds such as games and simulations.

Box 9.1

Check out Sensable Technologies's Phantom desktop haptic device at http://www.sensable.com and specifically the video of designing a hairdryer at mms://209.113.174.251/Broadcast/v8/1Intro.wmv.

Direct brain interfaces, which enable interaction with a computer by means of external brain-wave sensors attached on the surface of the skull or surgically implanted electronic chips, are also beginning to produce promising technologies for physically impaired learners. So, too, are eye-tracking devices and muscle movement sensor interfaces.

BLENDING THE OLD, THE NEW AND THE PREVIOUSLY IMPRACTICAL

There are various ways of conceptualizing blended learning but central to them all is an accommodation between the three elements: the 'old' traditional forms of learning and their environments (for example, tutorials, classrooms), the 'new' forms of e-Learning and the challenges of learning at a distance from the learning source. The reason why online e-Learning may not be taken up by sections of the educator community is, in some quarters, put down to organizational or professional inertia. This inertia implies that the tutors concerned are content to work as they have always done, unwilling to relinquish older, tried and tested means of learning and teaching in favour of e-Learning. However, there is much to be said for not fixing something that is not broken. If the tutors are confident that their traditional approach is effective and learners are picking up the knowledge, skills and understanding they need for the information age, then change is unnecessary. If they are *not* developing the necessary knowledge, skills and understanding then the situation is 'broken', and a radical review of pedagogy and content is required.

It is probably the case that very few tutors, perhaps a small minority of die-hard Luddites, would deny the benefits of enabling their students to engage with forms of e-Learning appropriate to their needs and the aspirations of the course. It is therefore always preferable to view the integration of online e-Learning as an enhancement and optimization of the learning environment. This is achieved by blending: taking the best features of each context and using them in a complementary manner that works better than any one of them on their own. As we argued earlier, though, e-Learning will progressively challenge the appropriateness and adequacy of traditional forms of learning environments (fixed times, places, curricula, content and pedagogies, and so on). Blending itself will therefore increasingly favour the more versatile aspects of e-Learning, which in turn will better accommodate, if not actually fully endorse, the distance education ideals of 'anywhere, anytime'. The routine features of many virtual learning environments already allow for easy distant access to the following 'traditional' context features:

- resource materials (repositories);
- work scheduling (personalized calendars);
- assignment submission ('drop-boxes');
- portfolio building (personal workspaces);
- mentor support ('hot-seating');
- tutor–student communication (email and instant messaging);
- communal learning (discussion forums, chat rooms, blogs, wikis);
- news and new topics (announcements);
- administration and progress monitoring (tutor/administrator spaces, accessible as appropriate to the individual learners).

Many of these features were previously impractical in distance education through radio, satellite and correspondence courses, though many worthy systems continue to meet a need where cabled and microwave technology has not yet conquered the huge distances involved in places such as the Australian outback. What is very much in its infancy at present in e-Learning, however, is the assessment of the learner's learning, where this is appropriate. It is clear that many learning activities, old or new, distance or local, are not appropriate for tests or assignment outputs.

CHALLENGES OF ASSESSMENT FOR ε-LEARNING

To a large extent reporting the results of assignment assessments and the marks or grades for tests (known as 'summative' assessments because they usually come after the completion of a learning programme) is a relatively simple form of output to deliver in an e-Learning environment. Some assessment formats may even be machine-marked and can give the illusion of the computer carrying out the assessment ('illusion' because clearly the tutor must provide the correct answers). The paramount example is the multiple-choice test, perhaps the simplest form for e-assessment, which can provide the basis of relatively sophisticated computer-adaptive testing systems. These systems build a profile of the learner's learning by setting test items, the answers to which can be collectively interpreted to judge how well they meet a set of achievement or mastery criteria. For example, if a secondary school student can consistently and successfully solve a series of two-variable equation items, the adaptive testing algorithm may direct them to the next stage in their learning, for example the solving of three-variable equations (ours is not to reason why!). However, if they are inconsistently successful with correct answers falling below a predeter-mined threshold, say 70 per cent of items, the adaptive system may direct them to additional tutorial work, guidance from their teacher and so on. In terms of achievement, the system will record factually that the successful student has mastered two-variable equations if more than 70 per cent of the items are answered correctly. Feedback is therefore generally restricted to mastery statements based on pre-set criteria.

Complex assessments such as the marking of essays, project assignments and so on are much more likely, however, to be carried out by the tutor, who will then post the result to each learner. The learner will quite reasonably expect any assessment to be meaningful, that is, to contribute to assisting them to progress in their learning. However, while the importance of feedback to a learner's motivation and next steps in learning is widely recognized, it is not so widely practised. Too many students regularly receive a summative grade or a mark, unaccompanied by any written or verbal narrative that gives meaning to the 'B' or the '62 per cent'. Even when feedback is given, it may suffer from the banality of brevity and cliché, for example, 'Well done' or 'Could do better'! Good pedagogical practice demands good feedback, to help students to identify strengths and weaknesses, and to scaffold their next steps. Such feedback has to be full, individualized and constructive.

e-Learning may fair no better if it falls into the traps of expediency with, for example, drop-down lists of prepared comments. In such systems a combination of the comments is selected by the tutor as a best fit for the summative feedback advice they wish to give. Automated – yes, convenient – yes, but pedagogically sound? – No. The alternative is to adopt the 'old' (but, we hasten to add, not necessarily widely used) summative methods of writing out a full feedback note or debriefing the student verbally. This is not difficult to deliver in an e-Learning context, but it may represent a challenge for tutors with pressing time problems relating to other important but time-consuming activities such as hot-seating, answering student queries by email and co-ordinating threads in discussion forums. Highly accurate voice recognition input may be an answer for the future but today's technology can certainly enable an audio file to be recorded as feedback. This can be done as the tutor assesses the work, for immediate storage and posting to the students concerned. However, it is probably worth pausing to reflect on how such off-the-cuff feedback, while convenient, also holds its dangers for ill-considered comment and, indeed, errors!

Formative assessment

Formative assessment, or assessment for learning (for a definition see Gardner, 2006: 2), is a form of assessment in which 'old' learning and teaching contexts still win hands down over asynchronous versions of e-Learning and distance learning. The learner in a traditional classroom should expect and receive formative feedback from their tutor during their learning, not just summatively after they have completed a programme. Again, we should acknowledge that not every traditional learning environment meets these expectations. Clearly assessment for learning is a difficult aspect of pedagogy for a lecture in front of 300 undergraduates but it is certainly considered good practice in smaller more manageable environments such as tutorial groups, school classrooms, seminars, laboratory practicals and training workshops. In essence, the tutor uses a combination of questions, analysis of answers, carefully selected, perhaps individualized tasks, observations of student behaviour (puzzlement, 'penny-dropping', and so on) and scaffolding prompts to engage each learner. The aim of the assessment is to establish where the learners have reached in their learning and to enable them to plan what steps to take next.

This is full-blown face-to-face synchronous interaction, with appropriate one-to-many interactions as the tutor also provides guidance on a group basis. Such a pedagogy is a huge design challenge for e-Learning. A human tutor, working online, could conceivably carry on one-to-one interactions on an instant messaging-based system, particularly a speech-based system. However, with more than a couple of students the intensity of activity would require a speed of thought and transaction that few would be able to accomplish and even fewer would find attractive. The prospects of an intelligent tutoring system gaining even a small proportion of the capability of a human tutor in such circumstances remain low, though expert systems and intelligent tutoring systems continue to improve year on year. So what is to be done?

Box 9.2

For a demonstration of the prospects of a computer system emulating a human tutor try out any Web-based version of ELIZA, a Turing machine persona. For example try http://www-ai.ijs.si/eliza/eliza.html. Although ELIZA is certainly not designed to be a human e-Learning tutor, it is still worth asking yourself if you would like 'someone' like ELIZA as a tutor!

One simple answer is to ensure that where possible the 'blend' includes the 'old' face-to-face engagement between tutor and learner. Rather than seeing such blends as tutors dragging their feet over innovation, the power of Vygotsky's 'more knowledgeable other' is nowhere better exemplified than in the traditional tutor–learner setting (classroom, tutorial and so on) in which assessment for learning is part of a sophisticated pedagogy. However, e-Learning actually does have a ready-made solution, which lies in the nature of the more knowledgeable other. One of the 10 principles of assessment for learning (ARG, 2002) is the enabling of self and peer assessment for students. The communal constructivism model for e-Learning provides a perfect platform for this, enabling peer-to-peer discourse that can obviously include supportive comment and feedback from other students. Some of these students will be 'more knowledgeable' in the area of learning that they and the other learners are following, and will act in the communal context as more knowledgeable others to scaffold the learning of their peers. The most able students may not find similar support among their peers but they can engage more reflectively on their own learning, especially with support from their e-Learning tutors.

MAKING COMMUNAL LEARNING ACCESSIBLE

At present, e-communities range from simple email lists to complex multi-faceted environments. Fundamentally they are a place for the members of the communities involved to communicate; and the technology continues to support a growing range of knowledge-creation and knowledge-sharing-options. The essence of any community is its members' sense of belonging, and very often the *raison d'être* is to provide members with information, contacts and support. By participating in an e-community, individuals can communicate with a potentially worldwide community of people who share their interests or needs. The process of participating is inevitably one that supports learning, either as a formal e-Learning environment or as an informal vehicle for discussion, debate, exploration of ideas and sources of information, from which learners incidentally or deliberately construct new knowledge for themselves. People learn in different ways and the wider the variety of techniques open to each learner the better the chances of success. However, a specific and sustaining element, which promotes learning, is the community basis and the communal constructivist processes that underpin it.

The benefits of communal constructivism fall to all participants in the community concerned, whether it is a formal learner–tutor system or an informal community of communicating citizens. The main benefits fall to the learners at whatever level and in whatever role they are participating. At present in traditional models of school or university education, the learner's role in the education system is something akin to a charity case. They receive the benefits of an education from the state (perhaps funded by benefactors such as their parents, if they are sufficiently advantaged) and they have very little input into what they learn. When, where and how they learn is also generally organized for them without any consultation or participation in the decision-making or design. Traditional education is arguably a spoon-feeding process, which has created passivity not only in the learners but within the whole system. Communal constructivism seeks to counter this by empowering learners to become active parts of a learning community, supporting their learning with shared expertise and shared knowledge creation, thereby allowing them to claim a role in their own education. In such a scenario the motivation of the learners to learn is increased and the learning process is made more meaningful.

Examples of ε-communities

There are many examples of e-Learning communities, varying from those with very specific special interests to those with a broad focus that might be as general as discussing world events. An example of the former includes the BirdForum (http://www.birdforum.net), a community of birdwatching enthusiasts who share a website with information, such as alerts and bird-watching sites, and email contacts and discussion forums for their members. The latter is well illustrated by one of the oldest e-communities, the Whole Earth 'Lectronic Link (The Well), founded in 1985 by Stewart Brand and Larry Brilliant. The community was designed to enable a dialogue between writers and readers of the *Whole Earth Review*.

Box 9.3

Check out The Well at http://www.well.com, which describes itself as follows: 'For twenty years, The WELL has been a literate watering hole for thinkers from all walks of life. The remarkable people who frequent this place include all kinds of artists, programmers, journalists, educators, activists and others who make a point of returning frequently to engage in discussion, swap information, express their convictions and greet their friends in the famous online forums known as Conferences.' Try out one of the open access conferences and see what you think.

Other e-communities are designed to support pedagogy, with resources and discussion forums for tutors in all levels of education. For example, the UK Teachers' TV (at http://www.teachers.tv) has some 580 downloadable video programmes of classroom activities and resources, with email feedback facilities on ideas and applications. The UK's Higher Education Academy (http://www.heacademy.ac.uk) is of a larger scale, managing resources, information, training and policy inputs in addition to supporting a variety of network discussion forums for the university sector.

How can communal learning be made more accessible?

At face value, the answer to this question is somewhat paradoxical, that is, the learning environment must be brought closer to the individual learner. However, while such an answer may appear to suggest that the community dimension should be lessened, what is actually implied is that the tools of the community's e-Learning environment should be more accessible to the individual. The primary examples of innovative new environments, which put the learners in significant control of their own participation, are 'blogs' (or weblogs) and 'wikis'. But before turning to these systems, it is worth considering how a VLE-type system might be made more learner-centred using the example of Fle3, the University of Helsinki's Future Learning Environment (ses http://fle3.uiahafi/).

Fle3 is primarily a Web-based system but can run over a local area network if necessary. It is designed to be as simple as possible in structure and boasts features that ensure the main emphasis is the learning process and the learner. Tutors and learners enjoy the same status, though the former do have access to an 'announcement blog', which is essentially an ideas-promoting device and scheduler to which everyone can respond. Each learner is provided with a 'webtop' (similar in concept to a personal computer's desktop) on which they can structure and store all their own resources, making them available to others as appropriate. They also have the facility to visit others' webtops.

There are two main tools for learners. The 'Knowledge Building' tool allows them to engage in groups that are working on the same topic or area of study, building new knowledge through discussion. The discussion is 'scaffolded' (in the sense of a structured framework) by a set of knowledge types that 'label the thinking mode of each discussion note'. The tool restricts access to the group from those who are not part of the topic study, enabling a secure environment for open discussion without the risk of external criticism. The second tool, called the 'Jamming' tool, allows digital artefacts to be created by the groups. These might be as simple as a text-based report or as complex as a multi media file comprising combinations of video, audio and images. At all times the knowledge creation tools and the extent and nature of participation are in the control of the learners.

Fle3 is one of the many high-quality systems that have emerged over the past decade or so, and which have been developed on an 'open source' basis. Open source organizations such as Linux Online (http://www.linux.org) and the Apache Software Foundation (http://www.apache.org) represent the epitome in collective learning and knowledge sharing. The source code for these world-leading systems is shared openly for continuous improvement by anyone. Many such organizations describe their work and outputs as 'copyleft' in opposition to what they call the 'closed source' mind-set of organizations that 'copyright' their products.

> ### 🖱 Box 9.4
>
> For a plain English definition of open source go to the Open Source Initiative website at http://www.opensource.org/docs/definition_plain.php. You might note in passing that although many open source proponents consider their work 'copyleft', the Open Source site itself carries a copyright notice!

The Apache and Linux open source sites are certainly accessible to competent programmers but most learners will look for accessible, ready-made environments within their own interest areas. For the large majority of people, then, weblogs (or blogs as they have come to be known) and wikis accommodate the main criteria for communal constructivist systems, that is, the facility to create knowledge and store it for sharing with others.

Blogs

There are estimated to be some 10 million blogs in existence (*Business Week*, 2005), all of them making the uploading of comments by users to be a very simple process within a fixed template. At first sight a blog looks more or less like a vertically scrolling Web page, with individual users' comments (their 'posts') presented separately and chronologically. However there is a degree of sophistication in their functionality, including, for example, the automatic 'pinging' of other post-senders, to alert them that a new post relating to theirs has been made, the 'tracking back' facility for showing who posted previous comments and the labelling of posts in specific topic categories. Only the blog owner (or owners) can set the theme of the blog discussions (this more or less distinguishes them from open discussion forums) with the predictable result that many blogs are self-indulgent platforms for someone's ego or for proselytizing a group's particular world view. Indeed, some of them do not allow participation and are therefore merely passive sources of information. In many such cases even the 'information' could be so idiosyncratic or personalized that it is not worth reading.

There has also been a growing tradition of political blogs, usually entrenched in either left or right-wing views. Examples include the well-established Andrew Sullivan blog, with a running commentary on US politics (http://andrewsullivan.com/), the similar (but politically different) Rathergate blog (http://www.rathergate.com), the UK Labour Party MP, Tom Watson's blog (http://www.tom-watson.co.uk/) and a Blogging the Beeb blog, which among other things argues a political bias on the part of the BBC (http://mediaprof.typepad.com/). While such blogs may enhance the learning of politics students and others with an interest in politics, it is likely that most people will find them a little too partisan to engage with them as a learning environment.

Less political and more educationally focused blogs might include the Scientific American blog (http://blog.sciam.com) and the multimedia (integrated images, MP3 files and so on) CultureVulture blog on the UK *Guardian* newspaper's site at http://blogs.guardian.co.uk/culturevulture/. Arguably the most effective wide-scale community impact to date has arisen in the more journalistic blogs, including the daily journals of 'bloggers' in difficult situations. Perhaps the most famous of these was Salam Pax, the pseudonym of the Iraqi blogger who journalled the progress of the invasion of Iraq at http://dear_raed.blogspot.com/. On general public interest issues, Ben Running's video blog of 14 September 2004, showing how a bicycle lock could be opened with a ball-point pen, prompted bicycle enthusiasts across the US to review their anti-theft measures:

> As companies have learned, the online hordes can quickly turn against them. Last September bike-lock manufacturer Kryptonite tried to downplay a blogger video that showed how to open its bike locks with a BIC pen. But the video instantly spread across the Net, forcing the company to spend more than $10 million on lock replacements. (Hof, 2005)

🔖 Box 9.5

View the actual posting on Ben Running's blog, http://thirdrate.com/testme/2004/09/14/, which prompted a US-wide public interest issue relating to bicycle security locks.

There are several blog-hosting sites that make it very easy to set up your own blog. One of the simplest is http://www.blogger.com. Go to the site and follow the simple instructions and in less than five minutes you will have your own blog up and running!

Wikis

In contrast to blogs, wikis accommodate the two main themes of communal constructivism with much more of a learning bent. According to Wikipedia, the first wiki was created by Ward Cunningham in 1995 and he is reputed to have taken the local name for the airport shuttle bus at Honolulu Airport in Hawaii. Meaning 'fast', Cunningham felt it a better name than 'quickweb', which his wiki system was. A wiki uses a simple database approach to create Web pages that are generally highly hyperlinked. An example of a sentence from Wikipedia illustrates the hyperlinking that is used to direct the reader (learner) to further sources of related information on the search word 'blackberry':

> *The blackberry is a widespread and well known shrub; a bramble*
> *fruit (Genus Rubus, Family Rosaceae) growing to 3m (10ft)*
> *and producing a soft-bodied fruit popular for use in desserts,*
> *jams and sometimes wine.*

The underlinings represent the hyperlinks to further information. Readers may well recognize the possibility of another meaning, that is, the Blackberry personal digital assistant. Wikipedia deals with possible ambiguities by directing the users to a 'disambiguation' page, allowing them to decide which meaning they want to track down (in this case the fruit, the PDA or 'the name of a *rabbit* in the novel *Watership Down*').

The two key attributes of a wiki are that the community of learners involved are free to create any definitions or narrative texts they wish, and that these definitions or narrative texts can be edited freely by anyone in that community. In the case of Wikipedia, the community is in fact the whole world, or at least the population of the world that speaks the language on which the particular variant is based (there are versions of Wikipedia in French, Portuguese, Spanish and so on). Anyone could go to the Wikipedia page for blackberry the fruit and add 'jellies' to the list of uses in the sentence above. This we did, and the change was registered in less than a minute. By the same token, someone could disagree entirely with the edit we have made and could re-edit and remove it. Indeed, there is always the prospect of a 'tit-for-tat' edit cycle between two or more contributors (but probably less likely in the context of blackberries!).

Wikipedia itself is perhaps the best known and most widely used wiki, created in 2001 by Jimmy Wales, a Florida dot.com entrepreneur. The system has enjoyed huge success: 'Some 5 million people a month visit the free online encyclopedia, whose more than 1.5 million entries in 200 languages by volunteer experts around the globe outnumber Encyclopedia Britannica's 120,000, with surprisingly high quality' (Hof, 2005).

⌐🖱 Box 9.6

To view another wiki, have a look at http://www.enpsychlopedia.com, a specialist pyschiatric site. Now find out what type of phobia Taijin Kyofusho is at http://psychcentral.com/psypsch/Taijin_Kyofusho. You probably will not have any edits to suggest but if you do, you will find that they can be achieved through a Wikipedia link.

There seems little doubt that wikis of both the specialist (for example, Enpsychlopedia) and generalist (Wikipedia) types will continue to grow as more people seek to learn from them and, crucially, from a communal constructivist viewpoint, seek to contribute their own expertise and knowledge, in the form of learning objects for others to use.

NEW CONVERGENCES

One of the most talked about new convergences on the horizon is often denoted by the equation

$$e + m = u$$

that is, e-Learning plus mobile computing = ubiquitous learning (sometimes also expressed as e-Learning plus m[obile]-learning). It seems clear that mobile computing (for example, PDAs) and ubiquitous computing (for example, wireless) will continue to show advances, especially with the strides being made in nano- and pico-technologies (where a nanometre is

10^{-9} and a pico-metre is 10^{-12} metres). However, it does not take much reflection on the issue to realize that there are significant problems to address as computing technology gets smaller. Screen size has always been a problem when it comes to miniaturization. Unless there is an adequate, eyesight-friendly projection of the visual output, the reduction in computer size to handheld mobile telephone sizes will probably remain attractive only for leisure or low-volume users.

What is needed in these days of vanishingly small computer technology, is something straight out of *Star Trek* or other sci-fi ventures. Regardless of what it might look like, such a 'something' must be capable of projecting onto a nearby surface with sufficient clarity and quality of presentation to enable ease of reading. Such technologies are certainly with us, with huge advances in wall-sized (including 3D) displays, near-to-eye systems and flexible electronic film or 'paper'. For everyone, but particularly the physically impaired, a realistic alternative is for the much reduced (in size) technology to 'speak' its contents and the learners to speak their requests. Whatever the future may hold, it is reasonable to argue that e + m = u may be a convergence in some senses but it will also cause a divergence, that is, mobility delivered in an ever-decreasing size will mean usability deteriorating to unattractive levels unless similar breakthroughs are created in display options.

THE FUTURE WEB: A 'COMMUNAL YOTTASPACE'

If computing power is increasing within a decreasing physical size of hardware, the very opposite is happening in the size of the Web. Estimates are notoriously dodgy but any reasonable attempt to carry out measures is usually much appreciated. Antonio Gulli (University of Pisa) and Alessio Signorini (University of Iowa) have produced the most authoritative estimates in recent times (Gulli and Signorini, 2005). Quoting other researchers' earlier estimates of 200 million pages for the four main search engines in 1997 – Hotbot, Altavista, Excite and Infoseek – and a lower bound of 800 million in 1998, they 'measured' the Web in January 2005 by analysing the terms used in Netscape's Open Directory Project (at http://DMOZ.org).

The Open Directory Project is itself a massive open source communal activity, aiming to create a 'comprehensive human edited directory of the

Web, compiled by a vast global community of volunteer editors'. Gulli and Signorini took the estimated 4 million pages of the Open Directory Project and identified 2.19 million terms in 75 languages. They created over 430,000 discrete queries for testing the Web and concluded that the 'visible' Web had over 11.5 billion pages, or approximately 1.15×10^{10} pages. Estimates of the invisible 'deep Web', that is, the Web pages behind firewalls and other security systems, are impossible to gauge authoritatively though some 'Weblore' (anecdotal) estimates would suggest upwards of 500 billion. We believe that such numbers are probably only a tiny proportion of the future size of the communal Web. As more and more people are empowered to contribute to the Web, its size will quickly know no bounds. Indeed, we feel that a reasonable estimate of the future Web should probably be measured on a truly astronomical scale. We have chosen to call this future Web, the 'Communal Yottaspace', where a yotta is the largest System Internationale (SI) numeric prefix, denoting a quantity of 10^{24} (approved by the international Conférence Générale des Poids et Mesures in 1991).

So we have the hardware technology being based on atomic-sized nano-technologies and we project an ever-increasing Web approaching the scale of a yottaspace, that is, a collection of 10^{24} resource pages. Granted that is 100,000 billion times more than the current estimated size of 11.5 billion pages (a 1.15 gigaspace), but as a metaphor for almost unlimited expansion we feel a yottaspace fits the bill! In time every person will have a miniaturized link to the Communal Yottaspace, truly giving anytime, anywhere access to almost boundless knowledge and to unrestricted opportunities to contribute to it themselves. Who knows what form this link might take but a PDA-type device with appropriate projection may well be a front runner.

SEMANTIC WEB

Fuelling this expansion in the future is at least one convergence that is already significantly under way, namely, the development of the Semantic Web. In simple terms, the development proposes a huge-scale categorization of all the material on the Web so that users may search it more efficiently. This categorization implies that instead of merely matching a keyword search to produce potentially millions of results of undetermined relevance for the person searching, a semantic version of the Web will allow 'meaningful' searching against Web resources that have 'meaningful' description tags.

Currently, search engines produce links to sites that simply have matching words or phrases, regardless of meaning. For example, using the present Web, a 0.42 second Google search for 'Loon bird description' reveals the prospect of some 140,000 results, which then await further analysis by the searcher. The first few pages might provide the information sought but there will also be 'results' that provide sources for such mismatches as Loon mobiles for children's cots, Loon fridge magnets and Loon ornaments that sing. Using a semantic version of the Web, the semantic search engine will 'know' a lot about the user's needs and inquiry context, and through time will 'learn' more. It will then create its own searching criteria to target the categorization that matches the 'meaning' of the search. Tim Berners-Lee and his colleagues have this vision for the Semantic Web: 'The Semantic Web will bring structure to the meaningful content of Web pages, creating an environment where software agents roaming from page to page can readily carry out sophisticated tasks for users'. They continue: 'The Semantic Web is not a separate Web but an extension of the current one, in which information is given well-defined meaning, better enabling computers and people to work in cooperation' (Berners-Lee et al., 2001).

In a sense the Semantic Web may be thought of as the next stage in a series that began with the Internet connecting computers and progressed to the Web connecting the resources. The Semantic Web puts a layer of interconnecting meanings across the resources. Clearly the whole enterprise needs standards that allow the data to be organized systematically as metadata, that is, data definitions that cover different types of data resources. There are a number of bodies, including Tim Berners-Lee's World Wide Web Foundation's W3C, the Dublin (Ohio) Core and the Institute of Electrical and Electronics Engineers (IEEE), working to ensure interoperability in the technology designed for the Web. According to Brian Mathews (2005) progress is being made, in the important digital libraries context, in establishing standards that are already usable on the Semantic Web (including the Dublin Core and the Publishing Requirements for Industry Standard Metadata, PRISM standards initiatives).

Mathews also sees 'four clear areas where there could be major implications for both teaching and research: in information management; in digital libraries; in support for interaction between virtual communities and collaborations; and in e-Learning methods and tools' (Mathews, 2005: 6). The first two, information management and digital libraries, are possibly the most obvious areas of significant impact, given that both are dependent on systematic data/information/knowledge resource labelling. Less obvious, perhaps, are the communal interactions and e-Learning but it is the convergence of the Semantic Web with e-Learning developments in a context of communal construction of new knowledge that we believe will be the key development in the medium-term future. The prospects for considerably more sophisticated knowledge development and sharing in a semantic Communal Yottaspace, served by increasingly powerful, mobile and ubiquitous computers, are simply enormous. e-Learning will evolve into new environments, which will exploit the flexibility and power that anywhere, anytime nanotechnologies will give to accessing the Communal Yottaspace. These will combine the best of the emerging communal learning features of such current systems as MOOs, blogs and wikis, and the more mature learner-centred aspects of VLEs and intelligent tutoring systems.

You may recall, however, that we earlier qualified the somewhat rosetinted views of the future by acknowledging that anytime, anywhere e-Learning is only possible where the technology is available and accessible. In the next section we remind ourselves that there is some way to go before e-Learning achieves the goal of being available to everyone.

ASPIRATIONS, ENTITLEMENTS AND RIGHTS

It is not an unreasonable aspiration to make high-quality learning available to anyone anywhere on the planet, given the relative ease of doing so, through the medium of online learning. In Western countries it is fast becoming a right of disadvantaged people to have access to the same services, including access to education in all its forms, as more advantaged citizens may have by virtue of their relative affluence, levels of family education and access to resources. However, it is clearly not the case in many parts of the world and even in the West there are many obstacles to the widespread access to e-Learning and Web resources.

In 1983, Brian Simpson, the then UK Education Adviser to IBM, used the concept of a 'ha-ha' to argue that many hidden obstacles lie in the path of

Figure 9.1 Looking beyond the ha-ha to a bright e-Learning future?

the computer replacing conventional teaching. A ha-ha is a sunken fence that allows uninterrupted views of a distant and tantalizing horizon but which prevents access to it (though in the land of its origin, South Africa, it prevented access by lions and tigers and so on to the lush lawns of country mansions without spoiling the view!).

Figure 9.1 illustrates the deceptive allure of e-Learning in circumstances where low levels of economic and physical resources can prevent access to it. In the cartoon, the tantalizing horizon is one of the bright future of e-Learning – with the local group working happily and others linked in from a distance. But for many the ha-ha is the continuous flow of inadequate funding, access, training and low levels of motivation and confidence that stand between some learners and the exciting future of education through e-Learning.

Such impediments are very real for disadvantaged areas and communities of the UK and other highly developed nations. Low bandwidth services in rural areas seriously restrict the opportunities of many learners at all levels of formal education and for lifelong learners through to the third age.

Disadvantaged inner-city communities, second language communities and specific ethnic groups such as travellers or new immigrant groups may find little in the way of resources to help even up the constraints on moving forward in their education, constraints that are often imposed by serious social problems. Physically or mentally impaired citizens, too, may suffer serious disadvantage if they are not provided with the assistive resources needed to level the employment playing field.

A FINAL WORD

If difficulties are real and tangible for citizens of highly developed countries such as the UK, they are much more visible and numerous for the citizens of developing nations. e-Learning policy should therefore continue to demand inclusive developments if aspirations are to move to their rightful place of entitlements and rights for all citizens of the world. If there are no insurmountable physical and design boundaries for information and communications technologies, then we should work towards a future in which every citizen of the world is enabled to contribute to global communal learning through the widest possible access to high-quality 'anywhere, anytime' e-Learning.

John Dewey argued, soon after the turn of the twentieth century (1916) that learning is a building process. We believe that education as a whole should be considered in the same light. There is much to construct and much to learn, and we believe that education will ultimately adopt and adapt to a communal constructivist approach, an approach that will be comprehensively facilitated by e-Learning.

References

Anderson, J.A. (1988) Cognitive styles and multicultural populations, *Journal of Teacher Education,* 39(1): 2–9.

ARG (2002) Assessment for learning: 10 principles, Assessment Reform Group, http://assessment-reform-group.org (also available at http://k1.ioe.ac.uk/tlrp/arg/CIE3.PDF).

Barnes, C. (1991) *Disabled People in Britain and Discrimination.* London: Hurst and Co. (in Association with the British Council of Organisations of Disabled People).

BBC News (2005) School creates its own Sim City, *BBC News*, 21 April, http://news.bbc.co.uk/1/hi/england/kent/4469189.stm

Becker, H.J. (2000) Findings from the Teaching, Learning and Computing Survey: is Larry Cuban right? *Education Policy Analysis Archives*, 8(51), http://epaa.asu.edu/epaa/v8n51/.

Bellis, B. (1969) *Computers and Schools: Interim Report*, Curriculum Paper 6, Scottish Education Department, Edinburgh: HMSO.

Benston, M.L. (1988) Women's voices/men's voices: technology as language, in C. Kramarae (ed.), *Technology and Women's Voices: Keeping in Touch.* New York: Routledge and Kegan Paul. pp. 15–28.

Berners-Lee, T., Hendler, J. and Lassila, O. (2001) The Semantic Web, *Scientific American*, available at: http://www.sciam.com/print_version.cfm?articleID=00048144–10D2–1C70–84A9809EC588EF21.

Blackhurst, A.E. and Edyburn, D.C. (2001) A brief history of special education technology, *Special Education Technology Practice*, 2(1): 21–36.

Bloom, B.S., Engelhart, M.D., Furst, E.J., Hill, W.H. and Krathwohl, D.R. (1956) *Taxonomy of Educational Objectives, Handbook 1: Cognitive Domain.* New York: McKay. (See also Bloom, B.S. (1965) *Taxonomy of Educational Objectives; the Classification of Educational Goals.* New York: McKay.)

Bush V. (1945) As we may think, *Atlantic Monthly*, July. 176(1) 101–108 http://www.theatlantic.com/doc/194507/bush

Cabinet Office (2004) *Enabling a Digitally United Kingdom: A Framework for Action.* London: Cabinet Office.

Callaghan, J. (1976) The Ruskin speech, *Times Educational Supplement*, 22 October, 72.

Carnegie Commission, (1972, published 1974) The fourth revolution – instructional technology in higher education, in *A Digest of Reports of the Carnegie Commission on Higher Education*. New York: McGraw-Hill.

Carter, J. and Jenkins, T. (2001) Where have all the girls gone? What entices female students to apply for computer science degrees, 2nd Annual Conference of the Learning and Teaching Support Network Centre (LTSN) for Information and Computer Sciences http://www.ics.itsn.ac.uk/pub/conf2001/index.htm

CCP (2005) The National Survey of Information Technology in US Higher Education, Campus Computing Project, http://www.campuscomputing.net/.

Chambers, A.C. (1997) *Has Technology Been Considered? A Guide for IEP Teams*. Reston, VA: Council for Exceptional Children.

Chisholm, I. (1996) Computer use in a multicultural classroom, *Journal of Research on Technology in Education*, 28(2): 162–75.

Collins, A., Brown, J.S. and Holum, A. (1991) Cognitive apprenticeship: making thinking visible, *American Educator*, 6–11: 38–46.

Collins, A., Brown, J.S. and Newman, S.E. (1989) Cognitive apprenticeship: teaching the crafts of reading, writing, and mathematics, in L.B. Resnick (ed.), *Knowing, Learning, and Instruction: Essays in Honor of Robert Glaser*. Hillsdale, NJ: Lawrence Erlbaum Associates. pp. 453–94.

Colwell, C., Scanlon, E. and Cooper, M. (2002) Using remote laboratories extend access to science and engineering, *Computers and Education*, 38(1–3): 65–76.

COM (2001) The eLearning Action Plan: designing tomorrow's education, Commission of the European Communities, 172 final, http://europa.eu.int/eur-lex/en/com/cnc/2001/com 2001_0172en01.pdf.

Crowder, N.A. (1960) Automatic tutoring by intrinsic programming, in A.A. Lumsdaine and R. Glaser (eds), *Teaching Machines and Programmed Learning: A Source Book*. Washington, DC: National Educational Association.

Cuban, L. (1993) Computers meet classroom: classroom wins, *Teachers College Record*, 95(2): 185–210.

Cuban, L. (2001) *Oversold and Underused: Computers in the Classroom*. Cambridge, MA: Harvard University Press.

de Ferranti, D., Perry, G.E., Sánchez-Páramo, C., Schady, N., Indermit S.G., Guasch, J.L. and Maloney, W.F., with Luthria, M. and Subramanian, P. (2003) Closing the gap in education and technology, World Bank, Latin and Caribbean Studies, Washington, DC: World Bank, http://wbln0018.worldbank.org/LAC/lacinfoclient.nsf/4145fb3d8bc4c82c85256739005396 62/69bf39cff4ab297985256d1000594d0c/$FILE/cover_index.pdf.

DES (1988) Education Reform Act, Department of Education and Science, http://www.opsi.gov.uk/acts/acts1988/Ukpga_19880040_en_1.htm.

Dewey, J. (1916) *Democracy and Education: an Introduction to the Philosophy of Education* New York: Macmillan

DfES (2003) *The Skills for Life Survey*. London: Department for Educations and Skills

Donald. J. (2002) *Learning to Think: Disciplinary Perspectives*. San Francisco, CA: Jossey-Bass.

ECDL (2006) European Computer Driving Licence, European Computer Driving Licence Foundation and British Computer Society, http://www.ecdl.co.uk/.

Economist (2005) How the internet killed the phone business, Leader article, *The Economist*, 17 September.

Edyburn, D.L. (2000a) 1999 in review: a synthesis of the special education technology literature, *Journal of Special Education Technology*, 15(1): 7–18.

Edyburn, D.L. (2000b) Collegial study groups: a strategy for creating shared visions of assistive technology outcomes, *Diagnostique*, 25(4): 327–48.

eEurope (2005) e-Learning: European targets and initiatives, http://europa.eu.int/information_society/eeurope/2005/all_about/elearning/index_en.htm.

Egan, K. (1974) Beyond linear and branched programmed instruction, *British Journal of Educational Technology*, 5(2): 36–58.

EU (2002) *eEurope 2005: An Information Society for All* 28.5.2002, Brussels,Com(2002)final http://europa.eu.int/information-society/eeurope/2002/news,library/documents/ eeurope2005/eeurope2005_en.pdf 263

EU (2006) Public health: ageing and lealth, European Commission, http://europa.eu.int/ comm/health/ph_information/dissemination/diseases/age_en.htm.

Evans, C. (1979) *The Mighty Micro*. London: Victor Gollancz.

Felder, R.M. and Soloman, B.A. (2005) Learning styles and strategies, http://www.ncsu.edu/ felder-public/ILSdir/styles.htm.

Finkelstein, V. (1992) Setting future agendas, keynote address presented at the Disability Research National Conference, Kensington, London, 1 June.

Fried, I. (2005) Gates: we're short of tech talent, ZDNET UK, http://news.zdnet.co.uk/ business/employment/0,39020648, 39209713,00.htm.

Gardner, J. (ed.) (2006) *Assessment and Learning*. London: Sage.

Gerard, R.W. (1967) *Computers and education. In Computers and Education*, New York: McGraw Hill, xi-xxi (first published in 1965, *Computers and education. In Computers: their Impact on Society*, American Federation of Information Processing Societies Conference Proceedings, 27(2) 11–16).

Global Reach (2005) Online language populations for September 2004, http://global-reach.biz/globstats/index.php3.

Gobee, O.P. (2005) Learning objects cannot be free of context:proposal for an alternative format to achieve reusability, EdMedia 2005, http://athena.leidenuniv.nl/bb/icto/content_docs/ presentaties/edmedia2005papergobee.pdf.

Gorski, P. (2001) *Multicultural Education and the Internet: Intersections and Integrations*. Boston, MA: McGraw-Hill.

Gulli, A. and Signorini, A. (2005) The indexable Web is more than 11.5 billion pages, paper presented at http://www 2005, Chiba, Japan and available at http://www.cs.uiowa.edu/~ asignori/web-size/size-indexable-web.pdf.

Hager, R.M. and Smith, D. (2003) The public school's special education system as an assistive technology funding source: the cutting edge, Neighbourhood Legal Services, Inc., http://www.nls.org/specedat.htm.

Haines, L. and Sanche, B. (2000) Assessment models and software support for assistive technology teams, *Diagnostique*, 25(3): 291–306.

Heeks, R. (2001) *Understanding e-Governance for Development: i-Government Working Paper Series*, Working Paper No. 11, Manchester: University of Manchester.

Hepp, P.K., Hinostroza, E.S., Laval, E.M. and Rehbein, L.F. (2004) Technology in Schools: Education, ICT and the Knowledge Society, http://www1.worldbank.org/education/pdf/ ICT_report_oct04a.pdf.

Hof, R. (2005) The power of us, *Business Week*, 20 June. http://www.businessweek.com/ magazine/content/05-25/b3938601.htm.

Holmes, B. (1999) Cross-cultural differences of use of information technology in education: a comparative study of the use of computers in Japanese and British classrooms, PhD thesis, University of Cambridge, Department of Education.

Holmes, B., Field, M. and Mikhailovna, S. (1999) The other in the mirror: student perception and identity in on-line Japan, paper presented at CAL99: Virtuality in Education: What are the Future Educational Contexts? London, March.

Holmes, B., Tangney, B., FitzGibbon, A., Savage, T. and Meehan, S. (2001) Communal constructivism: students constructing learning for as well as with others, in J. Price, D. Willis,

N.E. Davis and J. Willis (eds), *Proceedings of the 12th International Conference of the Society for Information Technology and Teacher Education (SITE 2001)*, pp. 3114–9.

HM Treasury (2005) Delivering high quality public services, Section 6 *Budget 2005*, London: HM Treasury.

IDEA (2005) *eGovernment: Reaching Socially Excluded Groups?* London: Improvement and Development Agency.

Individuals with Disabilities Education Act (1997) IDeA'97 Amendments, Final Regulations http://www.ed.gov/offices/OSERS/Policy/IDEA/index.html.

Jalili, F.A. (1989) A cross-cultural comparative analysis of the learning styles and field dependence/independence characteristics of selected fourth- and sixth-grade students of Afro, Chinese, Greek, and Mexican-American heritage, unpublished doctoral dissertation, St. John's University, New York.

Johnson, D.W. and Johnson, R.T. (2002) *Meaningful Assessment: A Manageable and Cooperative Process*. Boston, MA: Allyn and Bacon.

Kay, A. and Goldberg, A. (1977) Personal dynamic media, *Computer*, 10(3): 31–41.

Kolb, D.A. (1984) *Experiential Learning: Experience as the Source of Learning and Development*. Englewood Cliffs, NJ: Prentice-Hall.

Kramarae, C. (1988) Gotta go Myrtle, technology's at the door, in C. Kramarae (ed.), *Technology and Women's Voices: Keeping in Touch*. New York: Routledge. pp. 1–14.

Lajoie, S.P. (ed.) (2000) *Computers as Cognitive Tools (vol. 2): No More Walls*. Mahwah, NJ: Lawrence Erlbaum Associates.

Lewin, K. (1948) *Resolving Social Conflicts: Selected Papers on Group Dynamics*, ed. W. Lewin. New York: Harper and Row.

Logan, M. (2005) Wiring women won't close the gap, Inter Press News Agency, 18 November 2005, http://www.ipsnews.net/news.asp?idnews=31084.

Lynch, P., Holmes, B. and Lawler, S. (2005) The blind leading the blind: how the vision-impaired community are using a virtual learning environment to build and share learning. *Proceedings of the Inclusion: Celebrating Diversity? International Special Education Conference. Inclusive and Supportive Education Congress (ISEC)*, http://www.isec2005.org.uk/isec/abstracts/papers_l/lynch_p.shtml.

McDonald, T. (2002) Instant messaging enterprise security ramps up, http://www.newsfactor.com/perl/story/18008.html.

McLoughlin, J.A. and Lewis, R.B. (2001) *Assessing Students with Special Needs.* (5th edn). Upper Saddle River, NJ: Prentice-Hall.

McLuhan, M. (1964) *The Medium is the Message in Understanding Media: The Extensions of Man*. New York: McGraw-Hill.

Mathews, B. (2005) Semantic Web technologies, JISC Technology and Standards Watch, Joint Information Systems Committee, http://www.jisc.ac.uk/index.cfm?name=techwatch_ic_reports2005_published#reports.

More, A.J. (1989) Native Indian learning styles: a review for researchers and teachers. *Journal of American Indian Education*, 28(4): 15–28.

Murphy, E. (1997) Constructivism: from philosophy tp practice, http://www.cdli.ca/~elmurphy/emurphy/cle3.html.

NC (2006a) Additional inclusion information for information and communication technology, National Curriculum Online, http://www.nc.uk.net/webdav/servlet/XRM?Page/@id=6010&Session/@id=D_7VaIgozzjlyLvFl0guBK&Subject/@id=3331.

NC (2006b) Inclusion: providing effective learning opportunities for all pupils, Examples for C/8b – ensuring access, National Curriculum Online, http://www.nc.uk.net/nc_resources/html/inclusion.shtml#C.

NCBI (2003) Knowledge economy for all. NCBI News 5 (2) http://www.ncbi.ie/news/2003/
NCBI_news_Mar_Apr_2003.pdf.

NCET (1969a) Working Paper 1: Computers for education, National Council for Educational
Technology, London.

NCET (1969b) Working Paper 2: Computer based learning: a programme for action, National
Council for Educational Technology, London.

NCET (1969c) Working Paper 3: Computer based learning: a programme for research and
development, National Council for Educational Technology, London.

NESTA (2005) Report 13: 14–19 and digital technologies: a review of research and projects
http://www.nestafuturelab.org/research/reviews/reviews_13/13_18.htm.

Newton, P. and Beck, E. (1993) Computing: an ideal occupation for women? in J. Beynon and
H. Mackay (eds), *Computers into Classrooms*. Philadelphia, PA: Falmer Press. pp. 130–46.

Nielsen, J. (2001) Beyond accessibility: treating users with disabilities as people, Alertbox,
http://www.useit.com/alertbox/20011111.html.

O'Callaghan, G. (2001) Cutting the strings in a wireless environment: an exploration of
learning tools created by students for students, http://www.gocallaghan.com/wireless/.

OECD (2000) *Knowledge Management in the Learning Society: Education and Skills*, Paris:
Centre for Educational Research and Innovation http://www.mszs.si/evrydice/pub/.ecd/
knowledge.pdf

Oliver, M. (1990) *The Politics of Disablement*. Basingstoke: Macmillan.

Oliver, M. (1996) *Understanding Disability: From Theory to Practice*. New York: St. Martin's
Press.

ONS (2005) Household Internet access data, Office for National Statistics, London, http://
www.statistics.gov.uk/statbase/explorer.asp?CTG=3&SL=4376&D=4722&DCT=32&DT=
32#4722.

Papert, S. (1984) Computer as mudpie, in D. Peterson (ed.), *Intelligent Schoolhouse:
Readings on Computers and Learning*. Reston, VA: Simon and Schuster.

Partnership for 21st Century Skills (2003) Learning for the 21st century: a report and mile
guide for 21st century skills, Partnership for 21st Century Skills, Washington, DC,
http://www.21stcenturyskills.org/.

Poupyrev, I., Maruyama S. and Rekimoto, J. (2002) Ambient Touch: Designing tactile interfaces for handheld devices, in UIST' 2002, ACM pp. 51–60.

Pressey, S.L. (1926) A simple apparatus which gives tests and scores – and teaches, *School
and Society*, 23(586): 373–6.

Ramasundaram, V., Grunwald, S., Mangeot, A., Comerford, N.B. and Bliss, C.M. (2005) Development of an environmental field laboratory, *Computers and Education*, 45(1): 21–34.

Reding, V. (2002) Combating digital illiteracy, promoting virtual campuses and virtual twinning of schools: the e-learning programme's aims (2004–2006), press release, IP/02/1932,
Brussels, 19 December.

Roschelle, J., Kaput, J., Stroup, W. and Kahn, T.M. (1998) Educational programming environments: exploring the promise of component architectures, *Journal of Interactive
Media in Education*, http://www-jime.open.ac.uk/98/6/.

Rousseau, J.-J. (1762) *Emile, or On Education*, para. 564, http://www.ilt.columbia.edu/
pedagogies/rousseau/index.html.

Salomon, G. and Perkins, D. (1998) Individual and social aspects of learning, http://
construct.haifa.ac.il/~gsalomon/new/.

Scardamalia, M. and Bereiter, C. (1996). Computer support for knowledge-building
communities, in T. Kotchmann (ed.), *CSCL: Theory and Practice of an Emerging
Paradigm*. Mahwah, NJ: Lawrence Erlbaum Associates.

Short, E. (2003) E-commerce and the Americans with Disabilities Act: failing to extend the ADA to the Internet in Access Now v. SouthWest Airlines. *Oklahoma Journal of Law and Technology,* 1 OKLA. J.L. & TECH. 5 (2003) (formerly 2003 OKJOLT REV. 5), http://www. okjolt.org/webdox/pdf/emilyshortebrief.pdf.

Skinner, B.F. (1984) The shame of American education, *American Journal of Psychology,* 39(9): 947–54.

Smith, M.K. (2002) Howard Gardner and multiple intelligences, Encyclopedia of Informal Education, http://www.infed.org/thinkers/gardner. htm

Steen, F. (2001) Wireless networking, http://www.educause.edu/ir/library/pdf/DEC0102.pdf.

Stonier, T. (1983) *The Wealth of Information.* London: Thames Methuen.

Suppes, P. (1966) The uses of computers in education, *Scientific American,* 215: 206–20.

Sutton, S.A. (1999) Conceptual design and deployment of a metadata framework for educational resources on the Internet, *Journal of the American Society for Information Science,* 50: 1182–1190.

Tapscot, D. (1998) *Growing up Digital: the Rise of the Net Generation.* New York: McGraw Hill.

Thorndike, E.L. (1912). *Education: A First Book.* New York: Macmillan.

Tofler, A. (1970) *Future Shock.* New York: Random House.

Torres, J.L., Trapero, J., Martos, F., Vazquez, G. and Fernández, A. (2002) Voice for Information Society Universal Access and Learning (VISUAL) Project, http://www.broadcastpapers.com/data/IBCSoluzionaVisual.pdf.

Turkle, S. (1984) *The Second Self: Computers and the Human Spirit.* New York: Simon and Schuster.

Turkle, S. (1994) Constructions and reconstructions of self in virtual reality: playing in the MUDs, *Mind, Culture and Activity,* 1(3): 158–67.

UH (2005) A hypertext history of instructional design, University of Houston, http://www.coe.uh.edu/courses/cuin6373/idhistory/index.html.

UK (2001) Use of the Internet: by age and gender, January, http://www.statistics.gov.uk/Stat Base/ssdataset.asp?vlnk=4469&Pos=1&ColRank=2&Rank=272.

UNESCO (2001) UNESCO Universal Declaration on Cultural Diversity, http://unesdoc. unesco.org/images/0012/001271/127160m.pdf.

USAID (2006) ICT in education, http://www.usaid.gov/our_work/economic_growth_and_ trade/info_technology/approach/education.html.

Vygotsky, L. (1978) *Mind and Society.* Cambridge, MA: Harvard University Press.

Warschauer, M. (2003) *Technology and Social Inclusion* Cambridge, MA: MIT Press.

Washington Post (2005) Home schooling's net effect: online offerings filling gaps in students' lessons (Nancy Trejos) 16 July, Section c, 1 (also available at http://www.cmacademy.org/db2/Visitor/news &article=12)

Watts, E.H., O'Brian, M. and Wojcik, B.W. (2004) Four models of assistive technology consideration: how do they compare to recommended educational assessment practices? *Journal of Special Education Technology,* 19(1): 43–56.

Webster's New Millennium Dictionary of English, Preview Edition (v.0.9.6) (2005) Long Beach, CA: Lexico Publishing Group.

Weizenbaum, J. (1984) *Computer Power and Human Reason.* Harmondsworth: Penguin (originally published in 1976, San Francisco, CA: W.H. Freeman)

WITSA (2004) World IT Spending Rebounds Thanks Largely to Developing World, World Information Technology and Services Alliance http://www.witsa.org/press/11-22-04DP-US-5.pdf

Wood, D., Bruner, J.S. and Ross, G. (1976) The role of tutoring in problem solving, Journal of Child Psychology and Psychiatry, and Allied Disciplines, 17: 89–100.

World of Science (2003) e-Learning comes to India's Bund UNESCO National Sciences Quarterly.

Zabala, J. (2002) Update of the SETT framework, http://www.joyzabala.com.

WEBSITES

net magazine forum, http://forum.netmag.co.uk/

Acadia University, http://www.acadiau.ca/advantage/

Accessible Communities for E-Business Project (ACE), http://www.inishnet.ie/

AchieveOnline, http://www.achieveonline.com.au/

ActiveWorlds Inc., http://www.activeworlds.com/edu/index.asp

Adobe Photoshop, http://www.adobe.com

AliWeb, http://www.aliweb.com

Air, 1000 Hz Legend album, http://www.air-10000hzlegend.com/2.htm

Andrew Sullivan blog on US politics, http://andrewsullivan.com/

Apache Software Foundation, http://www.apache.org

ARPANET on Wikipedia, http://en.wikipedia.org/wiki/Image:First-arpanet-imp-log.jpg

Australian government/World Bank Virtual Colombo Plan, http://www.ausaid.gov.au/keyaid/vcp.cfm

Australian Project Gutenberg, http://gutenberg.net.au/

Babel Fish website language translator, http://www.babelfish.altavista.com

BBC News, http://www.bbc.com/news/

BECTa Educational Software Database, http://besd.becta.org.uk/

Ben Running's blog, http://thirdrate.com/testme/2004/09/14/

Berners-Lee's original proposal to CERN, http://www.w3.org/History/1989/proposal.html

Berners-Lee's first website, http://www.w3.org/History/19921103-hypertext/hypertext/WWW/TheProject.html

BeST Basic electronic Surgical Training, The Royal College of Surgeons in Ireland, Harvard Medical International and Intuition, http://www.rcsi.ie/best/index.asp?id=27

Best WebQuests (Tom March), http://www.BestWebQuests.com

Bignosebird web design turorials, http://www.bignosebird.com/

BirdForum, http://www.birdforum.net

Blackboard, http://www.blackboard.com/

Blogger.com blog hosting site, http://www.blogger.com

Blogging the Beeb (BBC) blog, http://mediaprof.typepad.com/

Book of Kells, http://www.bookofkells.ie/

Boston tea party eyewitness account, http://www.historyplace.com/unitedstates/revolution/teaparty.htm

British Museum, http://www.thebritishmuseum.ac.uk/

Burrokeet Open Source learning objects tool, http://www.burrokeet.org

Carndean University, http://www.unext.com/

CEN/ISSS standards agreements, http://www.cenorm.be/isss

Classrooms of the Future, http://www.cotf.edu/ete/pbl.html

Classrooms of the Future, hurricane monitoring, http://www.cotf.edu/ete/modules/sevweath/swhurricanewatch.html

Classrooms of the Future, satellite tracking videos (NASA), http://www.cotf.edu/ete/modules/sevweath/swtrackingpreview.html

Commonwealth of Learning (COL), http://www.col.org/

CompassLearning Odyssey, http://www.compasslearning.com/

Computer History Museum, http://www.computerhistory.org/exhibits/Internet_history/

Conway's Game of Life, http://www.bitstorm.org/gameoflife/

Creation of Study Environments, http://www.staffs.ac.uk/COSE/

Creative Commons, http://creativecommons.org/license/

CultureVulture blog, http://blogs.guardian.co.uk/culturevulture/

Déjà vu – Pages from Those Days, http://www.dejavu.org/

Digital Divide Network, http://www.digitaldividenetwork.org

Dreamweaver, http://www.macromedia.com

Duxbury Braille outputs, http://www.duxburysystems.com/

Early Childhood Research and Practice Journal, http://ecrp.uiuc.edu/

ECDL for People with Disabilities, http://ecdl-pd.aib.uni-linz.ac.at_what_ECDLPD-is.html

Education Resources Information Centre (ERIC), http://www.eric.ed.gov

EduTools, http://www.edutools.info/about/index.jsp

ELIZA tutor, http://www-ai.ijs.si/eliza/eliza.html

Enlace Quiché, http://www.enlacequiche.org.gt/

Enpsychlopedia wiki, http://www.enpsychlopedia.com

eTandem Europa project, http://www.slf.ruhr-uni-bochum.de/etandem/etproj-en.html

European Information Society in 2010, http://europa.eu.int/information-society/eeurope/i2010/index_en.htm

Europe 2005 Action Plan, http://europa.eu.int/information_society/eeurope/2005/all about/action_plan/index_en.htm

European Standardization Organizations, http://www.eeurope-standards.org

FactMonster NASA facts, http://www.factmonster.com/ipka/A0193167.html

Fle3, University of Helsinki, http://fle3.uiah.fi/

Google Earth, http://earth.google.com/

Gorillaz, http://www.gorillaz.com/intro.html

Growing Up Digital (Don Tapscott), http://www.growingupdigital.com

Guardian newspaper, http://www.guardian.co.uk/

Gutenberg Writers' Guild, http://gutenberg.hwg.org/

Higher Education Academy, http://www.heacademy.ac.uk/

Hot Potatoes, free e-Learning accessories, web.uvic.ca/hrd/halfbaked/

HTML tutorial (Dave Kristula), http://www.davesite.com/webstation/html/

Humanities and Social Sciences Online (H-NET), http://www.h-net.msu.edu/

i-CASE business case studies, http://www.i-case.com/newweb/index.htm

IMS Global Learning Consortrum: BS 8788, http://www.imsglobal.org/pressreleases pro.31006

Jason Foundation for Education, http://www.jasonproject.org/

JAWS for Windows, http://www.freedomscientific.com

Journey North, http://www.learner.org/jnorth

Lavamind games and simulations, http://www.lavamind.com

Learning Disability Pride, http://www.ldpride.net/learningstyles.MI.htm

Learning style inventory (Felder and Soloman), http://www.ncsu.edu/felder-public/ILSdir/styles.htm

Learning style questionnaire (Soloman and Felder), http://www.engr.ncsu.edu/learning styles/ilsweb.html

Library and Archives of Canada, http://www.collectionscanada.ca/education/art/05060211_ e.html

Linux Online, http://www.linux.org

Living Internet, http://www.livingInternet.com/

Logo Survey, http://www.logosurvey.co.uk/

Lycos, http://www.lycos.com

Macromedia Director, http://www.macromedia.com

Mac VoiceOver interface, http://www.apple.com/macosx/features/voiceover/

Market Share, http://marketshare.hitslink.com/

Massachusetts Institute of Technology, OpenCourseware, http://ocw.mit.edu/index.html

Massachusetts Institute of Technology, 'Programmable Bricks', lcs.http://www.media.mit.edu/ groups/el/projects/legologo/

Microworlds (LCSI), http://www.microworlds.com/

Moodle, http://moodle.org/

Multimedia Educational Resource for Learning and Online Teaching (MERLOT), http://taste.merlot.org/

National History Museum, Mission Explore, http://www.nhm.ac.uk/kids-only/fun-games/ mission-explore/

Netscape Open Directory Project, http://DMOZ.org

Notschool Project, http://www.notschool.net

Open Source Initiative, http://www.opensource.org/docs/definition_plain.php

Open University, http://www.open.ac.uk/about/ou/

Opera 8, http://www.opera.com/

Partnership for 21st Century Skills, http://www.21stcenturyskills.org/

Perseus, http://www.perseus.tufts.edu/

Philadelphia city government, http://www.phila.gov/wireless/briefing.html

Plato, http://www.plato.com

PostNuke, http://www.postnuke.com/

Project Gutenberg, http://http://www.gutenberg.org/

Psychcentral wiki, http://psychcentral.com/psypsch/Taijin_Kyofusho

Public Broadcasting Service, http://www.pbs.org/wnet/gperf/education/ed_mi_overview.html

Rathergate blog on US politics, http://www.rathergate.com

ReadPlease text-to-speech tool, http://www.readplease.com

Salam Pax blog, http://dear_raed.blogspot.com/

Saskatoon Public School Division, http://olc.spsd.sk.ca/DE/PD/instr/strats/drill/index.html

SchMOOze University, http://schmooze.hunter.cuny.edu/

Schubert WebQuest, schubertquest.tripod.com/index.html

Scientific American blog, http://blog.sciam.com

Scottish Cultural Resources across the Network (SCRAN), http://www.scran.ac.uk

Sensable Technologies: hairdryer design video, mms://209.113.174.251/Broadcast/v8/1Intro. wmv

Sensable Technologies: haptic devices, http://www.sensable.com

Sharable Content Object Reference Model (SCORM), http://www.adlnet.org

SimCity, http://simcity.ea.com/

Skinner Foundation, http://www.bfskinner.org

Skype, http://www.skype.com/helloagain.html

Smithsonian Institution, http://www.si.edu/

Social Assistance for/with the Visually Impaired (SAVI) project, http://www.formatex.org/micte 2005/241.pdf

Sony Computer Science Lab, http://www.csl.sony.co.jp/perspective_e.html

Stanford Online, http://scpd.stanford.edu/scpd/about/delivery/

SuccessMaker, http://www.rm.com

Supernova screen reader and Braille system, http://www.dolphincomputeraccess.com/

Tapped in, a virtual learning environment designed for teachers, http://www.tappedin.org/

Teachers Evaluating Educational Multimedia (TEEM), http://http://www.teem.org.uk/

Teachers' TV, http://www.teachers.tv

Techdis web design advice, http://www.techdis.ac.uk/index.php?p=1_3

Telediscount, http://www.telediscount.co.uk

The Inclusive Learning Exchange (TILE), http://www.barrierfree.ca/tile/

The Well, http://www.well.com

Timeline of Art History, Metropolitan Museum of Art, http://www.metmuseum.org/toah/splash.htm

Tom Watson blog on UK politics, http://www.tom-watson.co.uk/

Trinity College, Dublin, http://www.tcd.ie/CAPSL/clt/

University of Colorado, physics education, http://www.colorado.edu/physics/phet/simulations-base.html

University of Florida, virtual field study, http://3dmodel.ifas.ufl.edu

University of Houston, A Hypertext History of Instructional Design, http://www.coe.uh.edu/courses/cuin6373/idhistory/Pressey

University of Massachusetts: Aninal Watch http://ccbit.cs.umass.edu/ccbit/

University of Phoenix, online learning, http://www.phoenix.edu/online_learning/

University of Washington, audio description, http://www.washington.edu/accessit/articles?79

Virtual High School, http://www.govhs.org/website.nsf

Visually-Impaired Computer Society of Ireland (VICS), http://www.iol.ie/~vics/

Voice eXtensible Mark-up Language (VXML), http://www.vxml.org/

VoiceXML Forum, http://www.voicexml.org/overview.html

Web Accessibility Initiative (WAI), http://www.w3.org/WAI/

WebCrawler, http://www.webcrawler.com

WebCT, http://www.webct.com/

WebQuests, http://webquest.org/

Web Style Guide (Patrick Lynch and Sarah Horton), http://www.webstyleguide.com/

Web Weaver EZ, http://www.mcwebsoftware.com/wwez/

WebXACT website usability tool, http://webxact.watchfire.com/

Wikipedia WebQuest definition http://en.wikipedia.org/wiki/webq

World Wide Web Consortium (W3C), http://www.w3.org/

Zoomtext screen magnifier, http://www.aisquared.com/index.cfm

Index

Added to a page number 'f' denotes a figure and 't' denotes a table.

542016